The Children's Crusade

A play

Paul Thompson

Scenario devised in collaboration with
Ron Daniels

Music by
Robert Campbell

Samuel French — London
New York - Toronto - Hollywood

ISBN 0 573 05096 1

Please see page iv for further copyright information

The Children's Crusade was originally published by Heinemann Educational Books

Cast of the National Youth Theatre Production

The first production of *The Children's Crusade* took place at the Cockpit Theatre, London, on 10th September 1973, directed by Ron Daniels and performed by the National Youth Theatre with the following cast:

Sebastian Baker, Richard Barnett, Tom Bowles, Stephen Brigden, Gary Brown, Nicholas Brummitt, William Buffery, Nicholas Cull, Andrew Cullinane, Dan Day-Lewis, Mark Dewison, Martin Dimery, Peter Elliot, John Ellis, Terry Ewen, Patrick Field, Nicholas Frost, Anthony Gouviea, Ian Hector, Richard Hill, Richard Huntley, Malcolm Hughes, Mathew Jacobs, Robert Jenkins, Alan Lidbetter, Jon Main, Timothy McInnery, Anthony Michalek-Bonza, Stephen Marley, Stephen Oliver, Rodney Pope, Stewart Richards, Clive Riches, Richard Rogers, Colin Ryan, Mohammed Saleh, Ray Salim, Peter Smith, Boris Smith, Steven Smith, Nicholas Sorensen, Joe Tonna, Neil Townsend, John Wells, Michael Wilcox, Andrew Wilde, Mark Williams, Paul Wines, Peter Whitehead, Marian Boyes, Nancy Browner, Debbie Farrington, Jane Filbee, Stephanie Jucker, Lesley Mathadon, Caroline Tubridy, Lindy White

COPYRIGHT INFORMATION

(See also page ii)

CHARACTERS

Pope Innocent III
The Old Crusader
Nicholas
Francis
A Farmer
Klaus, the Farmer's elder son
David, the Farmer's younger son
Simon
The Marquis of Montserrat
Mascola, the peasant leader
The Bishop of Genoa
Hugh Ferreus, a merchant
William Porcus, his colleague
The Bandit
The Auctioneer
A Merchant
Teacher
The Sultan Al Kamil
Cardinals, Senators, Citizens, Peasants, Clerks, Merchants, Children, Parents

SYNOPSIS OF SCENES

Historical Note

For two hundred years in the Middle Ages, Christian armies fought Muslim armies for possession of the Holy Land. These were not romantic conflicts, nor were they motivated solely by religion. To a large extent they were wars of conquest undertaken for economic and political ends.

Between 1095 and 1291 seven major Crusades set out from Europe. Of these, the Fourth Crusade (1202-1204) was a particularly vivid example of imperialist expansion masquerading as Christian duty.

Pope Innocent III's proclamation of this Crusade met with little response throughout Europe, but eventually a small army was gathered together, for which the Republic of Venice offered to provide ships. This army never reached the Holy Land. The Venetian merchants took them instead to the Christian cities of Zara and Constantinople; the Crusaders attacked both these cities, destroying Zara and occupying Constantinople, the capital of Christian civilization in the East. Venice thus obtained an enormous trading advantage over her rivals, and Rome also benefited from this corrupt and bloody expediton since it secured the unity of the Christian world for the next fifty years.

The Children's Crusade may be seen as a consequence of these shameful events. For in 1212 thousands of European children set out to win back the Cross by peaceful means, seeking to succeed where their fathers had failed.

In fact there were two Children's Crusades, both in 1212. The first began near Vendôme, in France, led by the twelve-year-old shepherd boy, Stephen of Cloyes. It seems that thousands of French children followed Stephen, believing him to be the recipient of a letter from Christ instructing him to organize a Crusade. The children marched around the countryside for weeks, carrying Stephen in a gaily decorated chair. They suffered the ridicule of their elders and the drought that affected the area at the time, until, finally, tired and hungry, they dispersed having achieved nothing.

Despite this total lack of achievement a considerable mythology grew up around this so-called Crusade. It was rumoured that Stephen met King Phillip at St Denis; that the children marched to Marseilles where they were tricked by two merchants, Hugo Ferreus and William Porcus, who offered them ships to the Holy Land and then sold them into slavery at Bougie in Algeria; that some of the children were bought by the Sultan Al Kamil; that others were taken to Baghdad and beheaded.

The second Children's Crusade was more significant. It began in Germany six months after the first. A young boy called Nicholas, who was apparently gifted with considerable powers of oratory and who used to preach on the steps of the Temple of the Three Kings in Cologne, was encouraged by his father to organize an army of children. About thirty thousand children, mainly from the agricultural classes, gathered in Cologne. Although the average age was probably about fifteen, there are reports that some of them were under eight years old. They marched down the Rhine valley and crossed the Alps by the Mont Cenis Pass. Many died en route; others were abducted as cheap labour; still others deserted as the hardships of the journey bacame too much for them. Of the thirty thousand who left Cologne, seven thousand reached the Italian city of Genoa. Here they expected the sea to open and when this did not happen their disillusionment was made all the more cruel by the hostility they received from the Genoese, who saw them as a threat to civic order.

The Crusade then split into factions. Some returned home, some stayed in Genoa, but the main body wandered throughout Italy to Pisa. Of these a few even reached Brindisi, hoping all the time that the miracle would happen — the sea would open and they would walk across to the Holy Land and win back the Cross. None but a handful ever returned to Cologne. The parents of the missing children, parents who had cheered as they set out, now turned on Nicholas's father and hanged him for leading their children to their deaths.

Myths and rumours were associated with this Crusade, as with its French predecessor. It was said that animals and birds followed the children; that the Crusaders had an audience with the Pope who would not release them from their vows; that they too were sold into slavery. It is almost impossible to separate the myth from the reality.

The Children's Crusades were strange and tragic episodes in European history. They were the product of an age of fervent religious enthusiasm in a continent rife with extraordinary sects.

The Play

The Children's Crusade is a combination of the two Crusades and is not intended to be an authentic account of the historical events. As far as possible the play should be treated as a modern subject — the story of a generation in revolt against the corrupt world of their elders.

The children set out on their journey full of idealism, innocence and optimism, but they are soon brought into conflict with the harsh political and economic realities of the world. At various points in the play the Crusaders are forced to take decisions (political, moral and philosophical) each of which tests their unity, until eventually factions grow up and splits occur, causing the final disintegration.

The characters of Nicholas, Francis, David and the Bandit each take differing political stances and it should be useful during rehearsal to discuss the validity of each. For example, the idealistic "love and peace" philosophy of Nicholas is challenged by the more practical Francis. David, on the other hand, begins as the naïve son of a small farmer but through his experience he comes to reject religion and develop an understanding of the Bandit's "anarchistic/guerrilla" position. In Scene 11 the Bandit's life is shown to be anything but romantic, with no room for impractical moral absolutes.

The scene titles are important and should be included in the programme of any production.

It must be made clear that, in Scene 7, Senator 4 is voicing his own prejudices and fears rather than giving an accurate description of the members of the cast. In fact the National Youth Theatre cast was multiracial.

Scenes 2, 4 and 9 contain areas for improvisation. The cast should be given an opportunity to develop characters and the scenes that they create may then be edited and written up during rehearsal. From the examples in the text it will be seen that the purpose is to establish storylines within the Crusade and to convey an "impression" of the reactions and relationships of the children. The improvisation sequences also enable the actors to relate to the content of the play and to make their own statement.

Any group working on *The Children's Crusade* should continually draw analogies with the present day and should be encouraged to develop a critical awareness of the society in which they live.

PAUL THOMPSON

PRODUCTION NOTES

The Children's Crusade was first produced at the Cockpit Theatre, London, as part of the 1973 National Youth Theatre Season. It was performed by a cast of fifty-seven boys and eight girls.

The play requires no scenery and very little need be spent on costume. The actors should use their everyday clothes and footwear, over which simple tabards or cloaks may be worn. These are useful to identify the different character groupings (Crusaders, Senators, Peasants, Cardinals) rather than to assist individual characterization. To spend time and money on elaborate sets and costumes would be to militate against the simplicity, the appeal and the relevance of the play.

For our production three acting areas were used: (i) the main deck — the central space around which the audience was seated on four sides; (ii) peripheral areas — three platforms behind sections of the audience; (iii) the balconies above the audience.

These areas were used either simultaneously or separately, depending not only on the specific requirements of each scene but also on those of the following scene. For example, it seemed to us that it would be interesting to keep the first two "Cardinals" scenes on the balconies above the audience, from here the Pope and the Cardinals could survey the world as if from a pulpit. The Senators (Scene 8) were also placed on the balconies, but this time merely because the two remaining areas were full of Crusaders and it would have been cumbersome to stage an exit of fifty actors only to have them re-enter for the arrival in Genoa. By simply dimming the lights on the Harvest scene and lifting them on the Senators we were able to overcome this problem.

There is no reason why another production should not employ a more straightforward form of staging (proscenium, thrust or in the round) provided that the action of the play can flow smoothly and without interruptions. It may be helpful for a producer to use different levels or rostra, not only to define locations but also to draw the audience's attention to a particular group of characters.

Lighting plays an important role in the production, acting almost as a "zoom" lens in a film camera, picking out different groups with isolated spots and then expanding again to give the audience the scene as a whole.

The improvisation sequences demand that the producer helps each actor to understand the importance of the "choices" that confront the Crusade. Each character should have a complete story-line; where he comes from, why he joined the Crusade, how he fared on the journey, why he decided to go with Nicholas, Francis or David.

When selecting those improvisations which will be incorporated in the final production, the producer should ask himself:

(a) which are the most imaginative, interesting, dramatic or comic as self-contained scenes?

(b) which provide the most interest, relevance or variety when taken as part of a whole sequence?

(c) which of the groups and relationships are capable of being sustained as one of the many sub plots?

(d) Does the improvisation involve actors who, if the sequence were to be cut, would be left with little else to do in the play?

In making the final selection the producer should rely upon his own judgement, of course, but he should also be guided by the wishes of the company as a whole.

We found in our production that once the actors began to feel the relevance of the story to their own lives, their commitment to the project was astonishing; it became *their* project, *their* production, for which they had enormous care and felt immense responsibility and pride.

The Children's Crusade is a story about growing up — of starting out in life full of ideals, strength and hope and gradually being weakened, corrupted from within and from without, disillusioned and destroyed in a society which values only the power of money.

Through the play the cast express their own hopes and ideals, they act out their own future destruction. This ritual turns full circle in the line of the final song when the actors remove their tabards and challenge the inevitability of this destruction — the world can be changed!

RON DANIELS

ACT I

SCENE 1

In a period of crisis and confusion Pope Innocent III proclaims the Fourth Crusade

Pope Innocent III and six Cardinals. The speeches are punctuated by loud bells and at certain points a crash of a gong

Pope You Christians who call yourselves Christian, you who are engaged in wars and quarrels one with another, you do most sinfully neglect the true and sacred field for your valour. Though we have all the cares of all the churches upon us, still our chief anxiety is for the liberation of the Lord's sepulchre in the Holy City of Jerusalem. The Sanctity, the wonder of the Land of Promise, the Land chosen of God, of this Land the foul Infidel is now lord!

Cardinal 1 The Holy Temple is become a den of thieves!

Cardinal 2 The Holy City, the dwelling place of devils!

Cardinal 3 The churches, even the Holy Sepulchre itself, are become stalls for cattle!

Cardinal 4 In the Land of Our Saviour, Christian men are massacred.

Cardinal 5 Christian women are ravished.

Cardinal 1   }
Cardinal 6   }   *(together)*   Children slaughtered within the Holy Precincts!

Cardinal 2 You Christian men, you make war upon each other, when you are called to be soldiers of Christ!

All Cardinals To fight for the Lord in the land of His birth!

Cardinal 3 The Saviour Himself shall be your leader.

Cardinal 4 He shall be your guide in battle.

Cardinal 5 You shall march from victory to victory.

All Cardinals In the Glory of His love!

The Old Crusader enters. He should stand in a separate area from the Cardinals. His style of speech should be low-key and naturalistic

Old Crusader From the very beginning we were in the hands of the Venetian merchants. We were unable to meet the full cost of our passage and so we had little choice but to comply with their wishes. They would not take us to the Holy Land, but took us instead to their rival merchant city of Zara. And there the Crusaders rushed through the whole city, seizing gold, silver, horses and mules, and looting the houses that were full of costly things. That was Zara. It was a Christian city.

Cardinal 6 The wealth of your enemies shall be yours.

Cardinal 4 You shall plunder their treasures.

Cardinal 2 You serve a commander who will not permit his troops to go hungry.

Cardinal 5 Nor will he deny you a just reward for your services.

Cardinal 1 There is no crime —

Cardinal 3 Murder.

Cardinal 2 Adultery.

Cardinal 4 Robbery.

Cardinal 6 Arson.

All Cardinals ——which shall not be redeemed by this act of obedience to God!

Old Crusader We never reached the Holy Land. The merchants would take us no farther than to Constantinople, the capital of Christian civilization in the East. The treasures of Constantinople, we consoled ourselves with the spoils of war. But the victory really belonged to Venice. The merchants had achieved what they had always sought ... commercial supremacy over all their rivals.

Pope Absolution for all sins. Absolution without penance to all who take up arms in this Sacred cause. We promise eternal life to all those who suffer the Glorious calamity of death in the Holy Land. For the Crusader shall pass at once into Paradise.

Cardinal 1 Let every city.

Cardinal 2 Every count.

Cardinal 4 Every baron.

Cardinal 3 Send forth an army of soldiers to rid the Holy Land for ever of the Usurping Infidel.

All Cardinals You are the soldiers of Christ! Our prayers are for your success.

Pope It is the will of God!

All Cardinals It is the will of God! It is the will of God! It is the will of God!

The Old Crusader exits

SCENE 2

Cologne 1212—German children respond to the corruption and failure
of the Fourth Crusade

*Two boys, aged about fifteen, are addressing a crowd of Children. The
Children are kneeling. Throughout the scene they should hum, creating a
ritualistic effect. This "drone" should swell at significant points in the
scene*

Nicholas (*arms outstretched, eyes closed*) I waited patiently for the Lord
and He came to me. I put my trust in Him and He received me. And into
my mouth He put a new song. (*He opens his eyes*) Children of Germany,
hear me — the Lord is come amongst us. Come, children of Cologne,
hear me for I have seen the Lord! Jesus came to me and stood beside me,
He held me by the hand. I have seen Him! He is golden! Golden like the
sun!

More Children enter

Praise God, you citizens of Cologne, and send your children out to me.
Praise God, you children of Cologne, for you shall see the Holy Land.
You shall reach Jerusalem! You shall win the Cross!

More Children enter

Francis We have seen our fathers fail. We have seen them betray their
Crusade. Merchants got rich! Noblemen grabbed land! But the Holy
Cross remains in the hands of the heathen. The rich are unworthy of the
Holy Land. Children of Germany, only you can triumph where your
fathers have failed. Your hands are not stained with blood! The Lord
calls you to join the Crusade!

Nicholas (*arms outstretched, eyes closed*) O Lord, forgive our fathers,
they have made this world a sinful place. (*He opens his eyes*) Jesus spoke
to me saying — "Go ye in peace unto Jerusalem and ye shall win the
Cross. For as you are young so are you innocent. As you are poor so are
you blessed. You shall need no weapons for I am with you, and my light
shall be by your side." Jesus will be our guide and our path shall be filled
with flowers. Butterflies will float above us, and the beasts of the field

will follow us. And when we reach the sea ... then shall God perform a miracle. The sea will part before us and we shall walk across to the Holy Land! Our eyes shall see Jerusalem. Our faith shall convert the heathen. And our love shall win back the One True Cross! Children of Germany, the Lord God of Hosts, Ruler of Heaven and Earth, has chosen you to be His soldiers of peace! No more wars! No more wars! We march in peace to the One True Cross!

Francis All who would follow Nicholas—step forward and take the vow! Join the Holy Crusade of Children!

One Boy steps forward and kneels before Nicholas

Nicholas (*swearing in the Boy*) Do you promise to Christ Our Lord and to all the Saints, that you will fulfil the Sacred Task entrusted to you, that you will go to Jerusalem, that you will win the Cross?

Boy 1 I do.

Nicholas Lord Jesus bless thy servant. Bless him and keep him safe always. Amen.

Another Boy steps forward. He kneels before Nicholas, who swears him in

Do you promise to Christ Our Lord and to all the Saints, that you will fulfil the Sacred Task entrusted to you, that you will go to Jerusalem, that you will win the Cross?

Boy 2 I do.

Nicholas Lord Jesus bless thy servant. Bless him and keep him safe always. Amen.

The vows ceremony continues as a silent mime. The ritualistic "humming" continues

"Leave-takings" — these scenes should develop from improvisations. Most of these scenes take place around the town square; they could be lit by individual spotlights

<u>Boy meets Girl</u>

John Is that Nicholas?

Lesley He's wonderful, isn't he?
John Are you going with him?
Lesley Yes.
John On your own? (*After a pause*) My name's John.

Mother and two Sons

Jane Goodbye, Martin.
Colin Goodbye, Mum.
Jane Goodbye, Colin. Shall I say anything to your father?
Martin No. Don't bother!

Two Brothers and a Stranger

Patrick Look, here's another one ... mugs!
Terry Is this the great gathering?
Patrick Here, are you going to walk through the water?
Terry We're going to Jerusalem, are you coming?
Steve Yeah.
Patrick (*to Terry*) Push off.

Four Shoemakers at work overlooking the gathering

Peter Cor! look at that. (*Pause*) Stuff this, let's go and join 'em.
Ross Yeah.
Nigel (*to Ray*) What do you say?
Ray What about the guv'nor?
Peter Sod the guv'nor. Where they're going there ain't no guv'nors.
Ray No guv'nors? ... That's marvellous.

Two Skivers

Andrew Are you going then?
Trevor No, too much walking.
Andrew It's better than working.
Trevor Yeah, that's a point.

Return to the two Brothers — "walk through water"

Steve Come on. Let's go!

Patrick No.
Steve Everyone else is going.
Patrick All right. Let's you and me walk through the water.

The Country Boy and the City Boy

Michael You're from the country, aren't you?
Tony How did you know?
Michael You won't get far with no shoes. Why are you going?
Tony No work. You?
Michael No jobs round here.

A Mother says goodbye to her Daughter and Son

Lindy It's a pilgrimage, it's not a war.
Debbie I'm frightened.
Lindy You've got your brother.
Jonathan (*looking at Nicholas*) We're with God.

The Old Crusader and two Boys enter

Old Crusader Look lads, I'll tell you this for nothing. Don't go.
Paul It'll be different this time.
Robert We're going in peace.
Old Crusader Yeah, I've heard that before — set out in peace, come
  home in pieces.
Paul Is that a joke?
Old Crusader I wish it was.

Joe, the late arrival, creeps into the square and kneels beside two Brothers

Joe I knew I'd be late. Ten days it took me to get here. I'm worn out before
  the journey starts.
Nick Where do you come from?
Joe Hamburg. You?
Nick We live here.
Joe You're lucky. Two hundred miles I've travelled. I'm knackered
  already.
Sebastian Do you want an apple?

Joe Who's he?
Nick My brother.
Sebastian I'm his brother.
Joe Ta. (*He munches the apple*)

Nicholas Lord Jesus have mercy on us thy children. Give us thy blessing as we set out in thy service. Help us to be worthy of Thee.

The humming stops

All We promise to Christ Our Lord and to all the Saints, that we shall do His Holy Will. That we shall live as He did live and go where He did go. We promise, unto *death*, that we shall fulfil the Sacred Task entrusted to us, that we shall go to Jerusalem, that we shall win the Cross.
Nicholas Amen.

Nicholas's Father approaches his son

Goodbye, Father.
Father Nicholas ... the Lord be with you.

They embrace

Nicholas He will, Father. He will.

Nicholas walks through the crowd. They are still kneeling, they reach out to touch him. Music introduction

Song: The Song of the Confidence of Youth

Stand aside, all you merchants and bankers.
Stand aside, all you compromised preachers.
Stand aside, all you soldiers of war.
We can see what you really stand for.

We have lived in your world of corruption.
We've seen more than you taught us to see.
Now we're no longer fooled by excuses.
We won't be what you want us to be.

> We are young and eternally hopeful,
> And hope is a powerful thing.
> We are young and although we're not perfect,
> At least we try and we never give in!

Four Boys bring in a chair. Nicholas sits in it

The children cheer as he is raised shoulder-high. They leave singing

Children: Stand aside, all you merchants and bankers
Stand aside, all you soldiers of war
Stand aside, you compromised preachers
We can see what you really stand for.

The Parents shake hands with Nicholas's Father. They wave to the Children and cheer as they leave

The Children exit

The Old Crusader watches it all and exits slowly in dismay

SCENE 3

In the Duchy of Suabia — Principles are put into practice

A farm near the Alps. Two sons are harnessed to their father's plough. The Farmer guides the plough as they complete one furrow, turn, and begin another. In the distance, we hear the sound of Children singing as the Crusade marches past. The boys stop

Farmer Keep moving.
Klaus (*the older son*) Come on.

They continue working

Farmer What we could do with now is a nice drop of rain. That'd dampen their spirits for 'em. (*After a pause*) I've had enough of all this. Up and down to the Holy Land. Who do they think they are? Trampling over my beans. The years I've put up with it. Can't they find another way through the Alps?

*When they complete this furrow, they stop. They have now reached the
spot where they left their jackets, food and water. They take a drink*

Half of 'em ain't Crusaders at all, you know. Vagrants. Beggars. Always
after something. They'd have the shirt off yer back if you let 'em.
David (*the younger son*) It's a sin not to help 'em.
Farmer Don't I know it.
David But they're children.
Farmer Then they ought to know better.
Klaus Let's get back to work.
David I shouldn't be working here. My place is over there, with them!
Farmer Your place is 'ere. Get moving.

They work. The song dies away

David (*stopping*) They've gone. They never came near us.
Farmer Keep going straight! How many times do I have to tell yer? Look
at it. A right bloody mess we're making here. (*After a pause*) Come on
now. A nice straight line.

They work in silence

David My back hurts.
Farmer Soon be finished.

They work in silence

Simon, a Crusader, enters and stands on the newly-ploughed section

Simon Hallo, friend.
Farmer I just done there!
Simon Sorry.
Farmer What do you want?
Simon Would you like to help the Crusade, sir?
Farmer Eh?... Look here, if it wasn't for me there wouldn't be no
Crusades. I keep 'em going.
Simon You're a good man. We've been on the road for a month, we're
tired and hungry.

Farmer What do you want?
Simon Water. If you have any.

David fetches the water and carries it towards them. The Farmer takes it from his son and gives it to Simon

Thank you sir. The Lord rewards those who help Crusaders.
Farmer And punishes them who don't. (*To his sons*) Back to work.

They start to work

Simon Excuse me, sir ...
Farmer (*stopping*) I thought so. Something else.
Simon Do you have any bread?
Farmer Yes, thanks. (*Pause. To Klaus*) Give him a slice.

David hurries to get bread and takes half a loaf to Simon

David Take me with you.
Farmer What was that?
David I want to go with you.
Farmer Get back. (*To Simon*) On your way!
David You can't make me!
Simon Your son wants to come with us.
Farmer He's staying here.
Simon When we marched down the Rhine Valley, crowds waved at us and cheered. They brought us food, they gave us shelter ——
Farmer He's my son.
Simon —— at every town, children flocked to us, *their* parents gave them up willingly.
Farmer I need my son.
Simon More than we need him?
David (*to the Farmer*) You don't need me. You've got Klaus. I'll run away. You can't stop me.
Farmer You won't.
Simon Why won't you let him go?
Farmer I need him! We're poor, we've given everything we can. We can't afford any more. I sold a horse, my ox ... what else?... My land? Should I give that up too? I need labour!

David There's nothing for me here. Your land goes to Klaus!
Farmer Look, David, why should you fight in a foreign land? You can serve God just as well here at home. If it was just a question of ... of crossing a stream, yes, I'd let you go willingly, happily. You could jump across! Wade through it if you like! But the Alps! You won't survive!... And if you reach the sea ... (*He turns to Simon*) God is everywhere, to you He may only be in Jerusalem, but to me He's here in Germany too!
David (*to Simon*) Let's go.
Farmer Wait! Put down the bread. Put it down! And the water.

Simon does so

Right. In my barn I've got a sack of grain, I was keeping it. I got blankets. (*To Klaus*) Go and get 'em.

Klaus hurries off

The Farmer collects the water and bag of food, and he lays them at Simon's feet

Take these. Now you can have all that and what's in my barn. Take my jacket, you must be cold in the mountains. (*He takes it off*) You can have all these. But leave me my son.
Simon Is that everything you have?
Farmer That's everything I have.
Simon I respect your sacrifice. It speaks well of the love you have for your son ...
Farmer You say you're hungry ... there's meat in there. A sack of grain. If you take him you get nothing. Understand? No food, nothing. Less than nothing — you take on another mouth to feed. (*Pause*) Now choose. My son or my goods?
Simon You have little understanding of our cause. First of all we are not going off to war, we go in peace to put an end to war. Secondly, we intend to make no compromises. We shall not repeat the mistakes our fathers made.
Farmer Choose!
Simon The choice is very easy. Your son.

This should be a difficult choice for the Farmer

Farmer Take him.
David I'm sorry, Father.
Farmer Go!

They exit

(*Shouting after them*) Yes. All you "pilgrims", you think you're so holy.
You think you're so bloody holy!... How is it then, that when you come
back you're just bandits?... Eh?... You tell me!

After a pause, Klaus enters with a sack and blankets

Klaus They've gone. You let him go? (*He puts down the sack and looks
at the food and water*) Now he'll starve, like the rest of 'em.

Silence

Farmer Indoors. It's starting to rain.

They exit

SCENE 4

The Alps — Difficulties are overcome

The Crusaders enter, singing

Song: The Song of Overcoming Difficulties

Crusaders There's not a thing that we don't know about these mountains,
We know that children cry when they're alone,
We have learned to live in terrible conditions,
But we learned that lesson, long ago, at home.
Now it's cold. Oh, how the night is freezing.
But there's nothing we can do to alter that.
There's no food. So now we shall go hungry.
But then again, that's just another fact.

There's not a thing that we don't know about these mountains,
We've seen the stains of blood beneath our feet,

But we know that in the end when we have nothing,
Our hope alone will keep us from defeat.

Now it's cold. Oh, how the night is freezing.
But there's nothing we can do to alter that.
There's no food. So now we shall go hungry.
But then again, that's just another fact.

During the last verse Nicholas enters, carried in his chair by four Attendants

When the song ends the Children sit down in groups around the stage. It is night, they huddle together for warmth. Francis goes to Nicholas who remains in his chair

Francis Here you are, Nicholas. (*He offers Nicholas some bread*)
Nicholas Is that the last of the bread? (*Pause*) You have it, Francis.
Francis No. It's more important that you eat. (*Pause*) Please.

Nicholas refuses the bread

Francis takes a lantern and leaves to review the "troops"

"Hardship scenes" — these scenes should be developed from improvisations

<u>Two Brothers</u>

Francis approaches Martin and Colin. Martin is crying

Colin Now what's the matter?
Martin Nothing!
Colin You should have stayed at home with Mum.

<u>A Boy and a Girl are nursing an exhausted Girl</u>

Lindy Just keep her warm.

Francis approaches

Francis Is she all right?
Lindy No, she isn't.
Francis Get her a blanket.
Bill Where from?
Francis Ask.

John and Lesley, the two Lovers, offer one of their blankets

John Here you are.
Bill What are you going to do?
Lesley We only need one.

Bill and Lindy cover up the sick Girl. Francis moves on

Francis approaches four boys huddled together (Andrew, Trevor, Paul and Robert)

Francis Have you had anything to eat?
Trevor No.
Francis Here. (*He gives them the remaining crust of bread*)
Andrew Better than nothing.

They eat furiously, Francis moves on

Francis approaches a Girl and a Boy; neither has a blanket

Stephanie (*To Peter*) It's warmer walking, isn't it?
Peter Yes.
Francis Haven't you got a blanket between you?
Peter No. Perhaps we could ... snuggle up together.
Francis Yes. (*to Stephanie*) Is that all right?
Stephanie Yes.

They cuddle up to each other. Francis moves on

Two Brothers under one blanket

Francis approaches someone covered by a blanket. He lifts up a corner of the blanket

Francis Good-night.

A head pops out

Richard 'Night.

Francis moves on. Another head pops out

Pip Good-night!

Francis smiles and moves on

<u>Brother and Sister</u>

Next to them is Dennis. He is injured; they have carried him

Francis (*to Dennis*) Are you all right?
Dennis (*crying*) Yeah, I'm all right.
Ian I'm carrying him.
Caroline (*to Francis*) How much farther is it?
Francis A long way yet.
Caroline How far?
Francis I don't know.
Caroline Nicholas knows though, doesn't he?
Francis We'll reach the sea. We'll reach Jerusalem.

Francis moves on

<u>Two Brothers</u>

Steve is crying with the cold, Patrick is trying to warm him

Patrick Quiet!

Steve is crying. Patrick rubs his hands

Francis How is he?

Pause. They ignore Francis

Can I help?

Pause

Get some sleep.

The light fades. Francis crosses to Nicholas who remains in his chair. Their scene takes place in a spotlight

Where are we, Nicholas?

Nicholas Here. (*Pause*) We are here.

Francis No ... How far is it?

Nicholas I don't know.

Francis Look, they're frightened. They're cold, they're hungry. We've brought them a long way, Nicholas, they trust us!... How can we ask them to go on?

Nicholas We must go on.

Francis How?

Nicholas Faith, Francis, faith. The faith that brought us this far. Hope. Love. We don't need anything else.

Francis Yes, but tomorrow ... if we find no food ... what then? They'll die.

Nicholas We are in the hands of the Lord Jesus. We are perfectly safe. Perfectly safe.

Francis But they'll die!... I'm frightened, Nicholas ... if we should fail ... we must *do* something.

Nicholas Sit down, Francis. Sit down.

Francis What can we *do*?

Nicholas Nothing. (*Pause*) Please sit down. (*Pause*) If you think we need help ... I'll pray for help.

Francis sits at Nicholas's feet, he puts his head in his lap. Nicholas strokes Francis's hair. The Lights slowly fade

"Hardship scenes" — continue as the Lights fade and the Children sleep

The Shoemakers

The four Boys are sleeping almost on top of one another. Ray coughs

Nigel For Christ's sake!
Peter Leave him alone, he's sick.
Ross Ssh!

Brother and Sister

Debbie tries to share Jonathan's blanket. He pulls it away from her. She begins to cry

Debbie (*crying*) Jonathan!

"Dream Sequences" — these scenes should develop from improvisations

Trevor (one of the "Skivers") dreams that he is being nailed to the Cross

Boy 1 He's about the right size. Got the nails?
Boy 2 Here.
Boy 1 Hammer?
Boy 3 Here.
Boy 1 Just put your arms out, lad.
Trevor No.
Boy 1 Your arms.
Trevor No!
Boy 1 We've been waiting for you.
Trevor No! No!!

They crucify him

The Sea Dream (the Country Boy and the City Boy)

Tony I've never seen the sea before.

They mime walking through the sea. A wave looms above them

Tony
Michael   (*together*) No! Stop!

They are submerged by the wave

Carrying the injured Boy

Ian has Dennis on his back. He and Caroline mime the action of walking with him

Caroline You can't carry him any farther.
Ian I have to.
Caroline He's much too heavy.
Ian No. Please don't say that.
Caroline Too heavy. Too heavy.
Ian No.
Caroline You've got to put him down.

Ian lets Dennis slide off his back. Ian stands up straight. He sighs deeply. Relieved, he continues walking

The Crucifixion Dream

Christ on the cross calls out, a Disciple tries to reach him. The Devil, in the form of a serpent, prevents the Disciple approaching the cross

Christ Eli, Eli lama sabachthani. Eli, Eli lama sabachthani.

The Disciple stretches forward to touch Christ. The serpent pulls him back

   Eli, Eli lama sabachthani. Eli, Eli lama sabachthani.

The Sensual Dream

Stephanie and Peter, who were huddling together for warmth, now kneel and face each other

Stephanie (*whispering*) I need you to keep me warm.
Peter (*whispering*) I need you to keep me warm.

They spread their arms. Their fingertips touch

Stephanie Keep me warm. Keep me warm.
Peter Warm. Warm.

They hold each other and begin to sway backwards and forwards

Stephanie ⎱ (*together*) Warm. Warm. Warm. Warm. Warm. Warm.
Peter ⎰

The Nightmare (the two Lovers, John and Lesley)

Lesley (*waking up screaming*) No! No!
John It's all right. It's all right. Go to sleep.

They settle down to sleep

Additional dream sequence from the 1974 National Youth Theatre production

Nicholas's Father appears in a dream

Nicholas's Father enters. He examines the sleeping children as if they were corpses on a battlefield. A light reveals the presence of the Cardinals looking down on him

Cardinal 1 What are you doing?
Father I'm looking for my son.
Cardinal 2 What's so special about your son?

Cardinal 2 begins to laugh quietly

Father Have you seen Nicholas?
Cardinal 3 Why did you let him go?
Father Nicholas!
Cardinal 4 What about the others?
Cardinal 5 Who is your son?

All the Cardinals are laughing loudly

Pope We don't know your son!
Father (*screaming*) Nicholas!

Nicholas's Father runs off

The laughter suddenly stops

Black-out

A spot comes up on Nicholas. The light begins to spread. It is dawn

Nicholas Lord God please help us.
Help us to overcome our difficulties.
Comfort the sick.
The lame, the hungry. Please comfort them Lord.
Give them the strength to carry on.
Help us dear Lord.
Help us to understand.
Amen.

People begin to wake

(*Waking Francis*) Francis.
Francis Mm? Mm?
Nicholas It's morning.
Francis What? Yes ... yes.
Nicholas We're leaving.
Francis Yes. We won't be able to go as far today. If we don't find any food
we'll never get there.
Nicholas Don't worry, Francis.
Francis Look at them, Nicholas.
Nicholas Yes.
Francis Nicholas ... do you ... do you think we could leave the chair? ...
Leave it here?
Nicholas Why?
Francis I think it might encourage them ... if you walk.
Nicholas Do you?
Francis Yes.
Nicholas Of course ... I'll walk if you think it best.
Francis (*to all*) We're leaving.

Most of the Children are awake now

Attendant 1 We're ready, Nicholas.

Nicholas Leave the chair. I shall continue on foot.

Attendant 2 What?

Attendant 1 No, we must carry you. You can't walk.

Francis Leave the chair here. You'll need all your strength.

Attendant 3 We want to carry him.

Crusader 1 I'll carry him.

Crusader 2 I'll do it.

Crusader 3 So long as we've got the chair, we've got something to follow.

Crusader 4 We've got to take it.

Crusader 5 Let me carry him.

The chant grows, becoming almost menacing

All The chair. The chair. The chair. The chair. The chair. The chair.

Attendant 4 Sit in the chair, Nicholas!

Francis nods to Nicholas. Nicholas sits in the chair. The chant stops

Francis Let's go.

The Attendants carry Nicholas in the chair. Everyone moves off. They sing

Song: The Song of Overcoming Difficulties

Crusaders   Our hope alone will keep us from defeat
Our hope alone will keep us from defeat
Our hope alone will keep us from defeat
Our hope alone will keep us from defeat

They exit

MIME SEQUENCE

A Boy has died. He lies alone on the empty stage

One of the children enters

He takes the shoes from the corpse and exits

SCENE 5

Rome — An infallible decision

Pope Innocent III and six Cardinals

Cardinal 1 Your Holiness, what do you intend to do about these children?

Cardinal 2 You must put a stop to it!

Cardinal 3 Tell them to go home.

Pope I see you've already framed your opinions on the subject. It seems you don't require our guidance.

Cardinal 3 But surely, you can't allow them to continue?

Pope Cardinal, these children shame us with their actions, they shame us all! While we slumber, they in their innocence set forth gaily!

Cardinal 4 With respect, Your Holiness, we do not slumber.

Pope Our own crusade has failed. We cannot deny that. It has failed!... Thanks to the wicked intervention of the merchants from Venice.

Cardinal 5 We did not know they would attack Christian cities.

Pope They took advantage of us! They were never interested in the Holy Land. They had no intention of taking the Crusaders there! (*Pause*) Those Venetians are ruled by self interest, they grab all the treasures of Constantinople and leave us with the headaches.

Cardinal 6 You Holiness, we do not dispute the wickedness of the city of Venice. We should all join you in loudly condemning their treachery ...

Pope It is a sad reflection of our time when the interests of Rome can be undermined by commercial men.

Cardinal 1 About the children, Your Holiness ...

Pope Ah yes, the children. Now here is an example of the true Christian spirit. Innocence, sacrifice, piety ...

Cardinal 2 Do you seriously intend to give them your blessing?

Pope If my information is correct, and that would be a rare thing these days, they are expecting the sea to divide before them. Then they shall cross to the Holy Land on foot and shall conquer the Infidel with their love alone. Their innocence shall succeed where our weapons have failed. (*Pause*) Mmm ... (*Pause*) Could we provide them with ships? (*Pause*) No ... no ... To pronounce a blessing on this ... this "tragic" pilgrimage, would be to hold ourselves up to ridicule. We can't support it.

Cardinal 3 So we send them home, back to Germany!

Pope You show a remarkable ignorance of history, Cardinal! If we do that we shall be asking for trouble. (*Pause*) These children believe they are acting on our behalf! If we turn against *them* ... then they will turn against *us*. This is what happens with "misguided" religious fervour. It is very easily transformed into anger, anger against the authority of the Church. Can you imagine what would happen? Thousands of impetuous children? ... It's a recipe for social disorder.

Cardinal 2 Then what do we do?

Pope Our duty is clear. We do nothing.

SCENE 6

Northern Italy — The ends and the means

The Marquis of Montserrat enters. Francis is at his side, David is with him. Behind them is a group of Children. Nicholas is not there

Marquis I'm quite prepared to leave the arrangements to you. Organize yourselves as you think best.

Francis Thank you.

Marquis What's this? (*He picks up some barley to test their knowledge*)

David (*coming forward*) Barley. (*He examines it*) Two-rowed barley. It's got short roots so you don't need deep-ploughing, a light soil. You test the ripeness with your fingernail, like that. You'll be using this for malting, I expect.

Marquis Probably, I don't take a personal interest in my estate, not to that extent. (*Pause*) Well, I'm sure you know what you're doing. You've seen the orchard, the vineyard. I'll leave you to get on with it.

David What about the people who normally do this work? Where are they?

Marquis Ah .. well, they're with the Duke of Savoy now. Yes, over there. I'm afraid they left me for him ... left me in the lurch, so to speak.

David I see.

Francis When do we get paid?

Marquis When you've finished. You get a meal every night, and ... er ... that's all. Any questions?

Francis No.

Marquis Jolly good, I'll leave you to it.

He exits

Francis Well done, David!
David The man's a fool. He doesn't deserve this land. It's not used
properly.
Francis Never mind. We're getting paid and that's all that counts right
now.

Nicholas and entourage enter. He is carried in his chair

It won't take us long, Nicholas.
Nicholas We shouldn't work! All this is keeping us from our duty.
Francis If we don't eat, we won't have the strength to get there. We must
work. (*Pause. To the Children*) Come on.

Nicholas watches as they work

MIME SEQUENCE

Barley Field
1. Some Children cut the barley with sickles
2. Others gather it and bind it into sheaves
3. Others build stacks with the sheaves

*They work in a steady rhythm, introducing sounds, swishes and clicks.
They hum a tune*

Orchard

The Children take up the rhythm and tune

1. Some children are picking apples
2. Others are filling baskets and sorting
3. Others are loading a wagon

The tune builds up

Vineyard

The Children take up the rhythm and tune

1. *Some children are picking grapes and filling baskets*
2. *Others carry the baskets to the yard*
3. *Others are treading the grapes*

The tune builds up. All around the theatre there is now purposeful activity, a strong steady rhythm of work, everybody humming and "aahing" a tune. Positive enjoyment in their labour

   Suddenly six Peasants enter, with cudgels, scythes, and pitchforks

Peasant Leader You kids, clear off! This is our work!

The work stops. Silence

   You heard me. Clear off!
Francis Who are you?
Peasant Leader Never mind who I am. You're taking our work away!
Peasant 1 Shove off!
David I'm sorry, but we understood no-one worked here. The man said he couldn't get anyone.
Peasant Leader Don't make me laugh.
David He said they'd gone to the Duke of Savoy.
Peasant 1 Lies! We always work here. All our families work here. We do the harvest and the threshing, that's six months' work!
Francis We're not threshing. Just the harvest. We'll be gone in a week.
Peasant 2 Oh yeah? You're taking the food out of our mouths!
Peasant 1 We need this work!
Francis So do we!

Pause

Peasant 2 Look, mate, nothing against you personally, but you know what he's doing, don't you? You don't know the Marquis of Montserrat like we know him. He's got you on the cheap. He's using you to get at us.

Francis Then your argument's with him.

Peasant Leader Don't get clever, sonny, we need this work, we rely on it.

Francis So do we! We're going to Jerusalem, to free the Holy Land. To baptize the Infidel. You're interfering with the will of God!

Peasant Leader What?

Peasant 1 What's he talking about?

The Peasants discuss the situation

David We can't take their work, Francis!

Crusader 1 No. They've got to get through the winter.

Francis What about us? We've got to get to the Holy Land.

Crusader 2 We need it more than they do.

Crusader 3 We've got to eat too!

Crusader 4 There's more of us, come on.

David We can't do it! It's their work! Can't you see what's happening?... Nicholas, tell them! (*Pause*) Come on, you must ... you can't just sit there!

Silence. Nicholas adopts his "Guru" pose

Francis We are working here. We need food! To get food we need money, to get money, we've *got* to work! Our task is to get to Jerusalem! Everything else comes second! — there's no choice ... work!

Silence. Francis approaches the Peasants

Peasant Leader Are you going?

Francis No.

Peasant Leader Well, you asked for this then, sonny.

A scuffle begins

   The Marquis enters

Marquis Mascola! Get off my land!

They stop

   Go on. Get going. And you, Simonetti. Off!

Peasant Leader What are these kids doing here?
Marquis They work here. I employ them!
Peasant Leader But we do this.
Peasant 1 (*to Peasant Leader*) Come on.

They start to go

Marquis If you don't clear off right now, you'll never work here again. This is my land, I do what I like with it. Clear off! Do you want to lose the threshing as well?
Peasant Leader All right ... But you wait, we'll never work for you again!

They exit

Marquis (*laughing*) You will, Mascola, you will. (*He laughs*) You need me and you know it!

Silence

(*To the Children*) Well, get on with it then.

The Marquis exits

David looks at the two "leaders". The children go back to work and finally David joins in too. Nicholas remains aloof

MIME SEQUENCE

Barley Field — Orchard — Vineyard

In total silence they repeat the same action, but this time with no co-ordination. No pleasure

SCENE 7

Genoa — An emergency meeting of the Senate

The Bishop of Genoa and eight Senators

Senator 1 Senators, it's not a question of what we *want* to do, it's a question of what we are *able* to do. This city just does not have the facilites to cope with an influx of thousands of children. To allow them to enter would precipitate a famine!

Senator 2 Rubbish!

Senator 1 I would normally choose to ignore that remark, coming as it does, from such a worthless source. But this time my ill-mannered friend has inadvertently pointed to yet another problem. Rubbish. The problem of sanitation. These children bring with them all kinds of diseases; they have been on the road for months, in conditions which are beyond my powers to describe. Many of them have died on the way ... and yet this house is seriously requested to debate the possibility of permitting them to enter into our city. Senators, is this how little you regard your city?

Senator 2 All you're concerned about is your purse. You've done damn all for this city!

Senator 3 If you're so philanthropic — why don't you put 'em up at your house?

Senator 2 Unlike you, my house is not so large and ostentatious as to accommodate that many people.

Ad lib

Bishop Order ... order!

Senator 1 It has been said that we have a duty to these children. Well, that's as may be ... certainly, they display admirable courage and devotion to the Christian principle ... but I would remind this assembly that our primary duty is as it always has been — to the citizens of Genoa. And in their name I maintain that we would be failing in our duty if we allowed these children to enter our city. Thank you.

Senator 4 We cannot forget that Frederick of Sicily is at war with Otho of Germany, and in this conflict the City of Genoa is aligned to the forces of Frederick through our devotion to His Holiness Pope Innocent III.

Senator 6 What's that got to do with it?

Senator 2 Stand down, you fool.

Senator 4 It has everything to do with it! I would ask you to consider, geographically, whereabouts this ... "Crusade" ... began. In Germany! Can we afford to overlook the possibility, and I admit, it may only be a possibility ... that these children are emissaries from Otho — sent to capture our city!

General laughter

You may laugh. You may laugh ... but if my fears should prove to be well-founded ... I hope you have prepared your answers for His Holiness the Pope!

Senator 2 I presume that contribution to the debate was intended as a joke!

Senator 4 You'll see if it's a joke in the morning. You'll see, when there are thousands of urchins, with blond hair, blue eyes, running up and down the streets of Genoa.

Senator 2 We shall direct our attention to the real problem that lies ahead and ignore the flights of fancy so typical of the previous speaker.

Senator 4 You'll see!

Senator 2 In the morning these children, in their innocence, are expecting the sea to open before them. May I suggest that when this miraculous occurrence fails to occur ... we shall have a riot on our hands. And we should be well advised to make plans for that riot, now. Do we know how many of them there are?

Senator 4 Twenty thousand!

Senator 5 Four!

Senator 1 Seven thousand!

Senator 7 Thirty thousand!

Senator 6 To prevent a riot ... surely we could provide them with ships?

Senator 1 Who can?

Senator 6 If the sea fails to open. We could make them an offer of transportation to ... well to a port where they might be more welcome.

Senator 1 Who'd have them?

Senator 3 Who'd pay for the ships?... They've got no money. Are you going to pay for it?

Bishop Senators, senators ... please! (*Pause*) There are no ships available.

Silence

Senator 5 If I may be permitted. I suggest that we look at this question *rationally* ... Where's the profit? Could our city conceivably *gain* from this experience?

Senator 4 No!

Senator 2 Could you gain from it you mean!

Senator 5 Gentlemen, if the Pope were to give his blessing to this "Pilgrimage". And if he saw that Genoa was doing what little the city could afford in order to help them. Then is it not possible that he might consider some reward ... shall we say in the form of tax relief! This could give us an enormous trading advantage over Venice!

Senator 2 Ridiculous! Such an argument contains so many "ifs" and "buts" that you may as well wish for the moon!... Indeed my distinguished friend is become — a lunatic! His greed's got the better of his reason!

Laughter

Bishop Order! Order! I must ask the House to curb its laughter. Time is short!

Senator 5 Time is money!

Senator 3 These children need to eat! They may well be dying of starvation...! We cannot provide them with work, so even the most unimaginative of you must surely see that crime will be inevitable. I'm not talking about the occasional pickpocket, a burglary here or there ... I'm talking of crime on a mammoth scale!... Huge gangs of organized criminals, robbers, prostitutes, violence ... the looting of public places ... rape! Subversion!

Senator 4 Anarchy!

Pause

Senator 3 Senators, we would be criminals ourselves if we allowed them anywhere near our beautiful city!

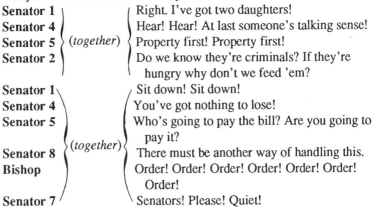

Senator 1
Senator 4
Senator 5 *(together)*
Senator 2

Right. I've got two daughters!
Hear! Hear! At last someone's talking sense!
Property first! Property first!
Do we know they're criminals? If they're hungry why don't we feed 'em?

Senator 1
Senator 4
Senator 5
Senator 8 *(together)*
Bishop
Senator 7

Sit down! Sit down!
You've got nothing to lose!
Who's going to pay the bill? Are you going to pay it?
There must be another way of handling this.
Order! Order! Order! Order! Order! Order! Order!
Senators! Please! Quiet!

Above the noise

Senator 3 If anything goes wrong — we are the ones responsible!

SCENE 8

Outside Genoa — the Senators welcome the Children

In a Spotlight — one Boy sings the first verse. The light spreads as other voices join in. The song builds to a celebration

Song: The Song of False Conclusions

Boy   I am!
             There is the sea.
             I am,
             At last I am free,
             To understand the cruel land,
             I left behind, on my journey

Crusaders We're here!
             We've reached the sea.
             We're here,
             We've reached the sea.
             We always knew what we could do,
             When we set out, on our journey.

             On the road where we've been,
             We have grown very wise,
             We have learned how to see
             You just open your eyes!

             And you look straight ahead!
             Where the sea meets the shore!
             We have done what we said!
             We don't doubt anymore!

             The sea. There is the sea!

Crusader 1 There's someone coming!

Crusader 2 Who is it? (*Pause*) There's three of them!

Crusader 4 Ssh ... They must be from the city.

Crusader 2 Perhaps they've come to welcome us. To bring us gifts. Presents!

General ad lib. Cheers! Shouts!

The Bishop, Senator 3 and Senator 4 enter

Bishop (*out of breath*) We come from the City of Genoa.

More cheers

Phew! It's a long way up here ... Quite a climb ... My goodness me, there's a lot of you.

Senator 4 You're telling me.

Bishop I am the Bishop of Genoa and these are two of our most distinguished citizens ... Tell me, who is your leader?

Francis Nicholas ... this way.

Francis leads them to Nicholas. The rest of the children sit down

Bishop Welcome, Nicholas.

The Bishop invites Nicholas to kiss his ring. Nicholas does nothing

Nicholas Thank you.

Uncomfortable pause

Bishop And welcome to you all! Your journey has earned the admiration of us all and we trust that your stay here will be a pleasant one! (*Pause*) How long do you intend to stay?

Nicholas Until the morning.

Bishop Ah, yes. The miracle.

Nicholas At dawn the sea will divide before us.

Senator 3 What if it doesn't happen?

Nicholas It will.

Senator 4 But ... what if it doesn't? What are your plans?

Nicholas God will not fail us. He has led us this far and He will lead us to the Holy Land.

Bishop But how do you know it was He who led you?

Nicholas We couldn't have done it without Him.

Pause

Bishop I see.

Senator 4 I'm afraid we must tell you that you will not be permitted to enter the walls of our city.

Crusader 1 Why not?

General ad lib. "Why not?" , "What's the matter?"

Bishop We don't wish to appear inhospitable ... but Genoa is very small and we just don't have the facilities. *(Pause)* We could however, arrange for small groups of you to ... er ... visit the city ... to admire the beauty of Genoa. I'm sure we could arrange that, couldn't we?

Crusader 3 What's the matter with us?

Crusader 1 Don't you want us?

Senator 3 I regret that this is the decision of the Senate. There's nothing we can do. You will be allowed to remain here for three days, and we shall do whatever we can to organize food and any other help.

Bishop Perhaps we might be able to look favourably on an application for permanent residence. *(Pause)* Provided there weren't too many of you, of course.

Nicholas No thank you. We accept your offer of the food but in the morning we shall be gone.

Bishop Thank you. *(To everybody)* And welcome once again! *(Pause. To Nicholas)* We just don't want any trouble, you understand?

Senator 4 Three days remember.

The Bishop and Senators exit in silence

Crusader 5 Bloody fine welcome that was!

David What did they think we were going to do? What are we, robbers? Bandits ...? The bastards!

Crusader 6 Some welcome!
Crusader 7 Who needs 'em!

General ad lib

Nicholas Who wants to see the merchant's city anyway? Their city may
  be very fine but it doesn't compare with Jerusalem!
Crusader 8 No! That's right!
Crusader 9 Right!

Cheers. Shouts. "Jerusalem!"

Francis Forget about the merchants! That's not what we came for! Get
  some sleep ...!We have a long way to go in the morning.

Silence. Some Children sit down, others stand in small groups

David brings the chair to Nicholas

David (*to Nicholas*) So now we wait for the morning.
Nicholas Turn my chair to the sea.

*Nicholas sits. All the Children look towards the sea. They hold their
positions in absolute silence*

The Lights fade — extremely slowly, to

BLACK-OUT

ACT II

SCENE 9

Outside Genoa — The question of survival

Two acting areas are required for this scene. The main acting area should be for scenes in the camp, and the other for scenes in Genoa

The Crusaders enter, having been to the sea for the twenty-seventh time. They sit or stand in groups around the camp

Meanwhile, the rest of the cast take up their positions for the Genoa sequence

Song: The Song of Survival

Crusaders   In the city down below
We can see why we left home
We can see the merchants bargaining all day
They fight like bitches
To grab more riches
And their wealth is tempting some of us away

In order to survive
You must simply stay alive
But for us this is how we'd like to live
You are my brother
We help each other
But in Genoa they take before they give

Genoa is too near to us
The city interferes with us
And 'though we're confused, we must not show it.
The city feeds us

But first it bleeds us
The Crusade is breaking up and we know it.

In Genoa—Children are begging for alms. The Citizens and Merchants refuse to help. The shouts should come from all directions

Girl 1 Alms. Alms. Alms for the Crusade!
Boy 1 Alms. Alms. Please help us!
Girl 2 Alms for the Crusade. Alms for the Crusade.
Merchant 1 You're getting nothing out of me!
Boy 2 Please help the Crusade!
Merchant 2 We've given enough!
Girl 1 Alms. Alms!
Boy 1 Alms for the Crusade!
Merchant 3 How much longer are you kids going to be here?
Merchant 4 Don't you kids ever wash?
Girl 3 Alms! Alms! Help the Crusade.
Merchant 5 I've got better things to do with my money.
Merchant 6 Bloody scroungers!
Merchant 4 Begging! You're always begging! Try working!
Girl 4 Please help us, sir. Alms for the Crusade.
Merchant 5 Beggars and thieves ... that's all you lot are!

The following scenes should develop from improvisations

Steve and Patrick are robbing a house

Terry, one of the Crusaders, approaches them

Terry What are you two doing?
Steve (*at the bottom of the ladder*) Oh nothing. What are you doing?
Terry Begging for the Crusade.
Steve Same here.

Terry notices Patrick descending the ladder with a sack

Terry Cor! Where did you get that?
Patrick Begging!
Terry Yeah? You didn't nick it, did you?

Patrick Push off!

Begging for alms

Girl 2 Alms for the Crusade. Alms!
Merchant 3 I've had enough of you lot. Clear off!
Girl 2 Alms! Please help the Crusade. Alms! Alms!

A Boy applies for a job with a Carpet-maker

Carpet-maker Our speciality is the imitation of carpets from the Orient.
Here you've got the Turkish and over there's the Persian. Do you know
the difference?
Boy No.
Carpet-maker Well, if you want to stay here and work as my apprentice
you'll have to learn. And you can start by taking that thing off.

The Boy takes off his Crusader costume

Begging for alms

Girl 3 Alms for the Crusade. Alms for the Crusade.
Merchant 4 Go somewhere else. Leave us alone!
Girl 3 Alms! Alms!

The Shoemakers have become Pickpockets.

The four Boys bump into a Merchant

Nigel Sorry, mister.
Merchant Here!
Peter ⎫   ⎧ Watch out.
Ross ⎬ (*together*)   ⎨ Don't push.
Ray   ⎭   ⎩ 'Scuse me.

Finally they sort themselves out. The Merchant continues on his way

Merchant Ill-mannered lice.

He exits

Peter Did you get it?
Ray Yeah! (*He holds the stolen purse*)

Begging for alms

Boy Alms! Alms! Please help us.
Girl 1 Help the Crusade. Help the Crusade.
Girl 2 Alms! Alms! Alms!

A Girl begs, a Boy steals ... their relationship ends

Stephanie Alms for the Crusade.
Peter (*coming up to her*) You're not still at that, are you? Look at this.

He shows her a copper jug

Stephanie Where did you get that?
Peter Well, I didn't get it begging.
Stephanie You stole it?
Peter Yeah. So what?
Stephanie So what?!
Peter Come off it, I've had enough of "preaching".
Stephanie You're a thief!

Pause

Peter Well, sod you, then.

He goes

Stephanie (*after a pause*) Alms for the Crusade. Alms for the Crusade.
Please help the Crusade.

The two Lovers rent a house

John That's fine. We'll take it.
Landlord Just the two of you? No children?
Lesley Not yet.
Landlord Not pregnant, are you?

Lesley No.

Pause

Landlord You were with the Crusade, weren't you?... Well, just remember, this is a respectable house. You've got a job?
John Yes.
Landlord Well, give us the rent then.

Begging for alms

Girl 3 Alms! Alms! Help the Crusade. Help the Crusade.
Merchant 1 Why don't you work for a living like everyone else?
Girl 3 Alms for the Crusade.

The Country Boy and the City Boy apply for a job at a bank

Banker Secure employment, excellent prospects, and reasonable remuneration ... does that appeal to you?
Michael Yes.
Tony Yes. I've always wanted to work in a bank.
Banker (*to Michael*) You can start as a messenger.
Michael What about him?
Banker I'm afraid I can only offer you employment.

Pause

Michael No thank you.

Begging for alms

Boy 2 Alms! Alms! Please help us!
Merchant 3 I'm fed up with you lot! Go away!
Boy 2 Help the Crusade!

A Girl turns to prostitution

Debbie Hallo.
Merchant 6 Bit young?

Debbie I ...
Merchant 6 Five marks. Five.
Debbie Yes.

He puts his arm around her. They leave

The Camp outside Genoa—these scenes should develop from improvisations

The Children are sitting around in small groups

Pedlar 1 (*off*) Buns and cakes. Buns and cakes.
Pedlar 2 (*off*) Meat pies! Meat pies!
Pedlar 1 (*off*) Newly baked! Newly baked! Come and get your buns and
  cakes!

Two Boys picking up litter

Boy 1 Nothing but complaints, that's all we get.
Boy 2 Yeah. Look at this lot.
Boy 2 Funny how people change.
Pedlar 2 (*off*) Who will buy—lovely meat pies? Who will buy — lovely
  meat pies?
Pedlar 1 (*off*) Buns and cakes. Buns and cakes.

Two Skivers

Trevor is sitting down

Andy returns from the city

Andy There's two jobs going at the bakery. He'll see us in the morning.
Trevor What? Work?
Andy Come on ... it's better than all this waiting.

A Girl enters the camp and puts some money in the coffer

Francis (*to Marian*) Thank you.

Brother and sister

Marian returns from Genoa to her brother, Stewart

Stewart Where have you been?

Pause

   You slag.
Marian What else can I do?
Stewart Just look at you.

Stephanie returns to the camp. She puts some money into the coffer

Francis (*to Stephanie*) Thank you.

Stephanie finds somewhere to sit alone

Lindy and Bill are counting the "collection"

Francis How much have we collected?
Lindy Less than yesterday.
Bill Perhaps we should send more people out begging.
Lindy I think they've had enough of us.

   The two Pedlars enter

Pedlar 1 Newly baked. Buns and cakes!
Pedlar 2 Who will buy? Lovely meat pies! Who will buy? Lovely meat
   pies!... Do you want a meat pie, Sunshine?
Boy Shove off.
Pedlar 2 Suit yourself. Meat pies! Meat pies!

David approaches the Pedlars

David (*to Pedlar 2*) Clear off! Go on, get out of here!
Pedlar 1 Buns and cakes!
David (*to Pedlar 1*) And you ... clear off!

David pushes them off

Vultures.

The Pedlars exit

The Boys sitting in a group near David

Boy 1 I've had enough of all this ... down to the sea everyday. Watch the tide come in, the tide go out. It's daft.
Boy 2 What else can we do?
Boy 1 I'm not going through all that tomorrow. I'm staying here.
Boy 2 I'm still going.
David We must go to the sea.
Boy 3 But nothing happens.
David We must go every day.

Pedlar 2 returns

Pedlar 2 (*quietly*) Meat pies? Meat pies ...? Who wants a meat pie?

A Boy approaches. This should be one of the Boys who has been stealing in Genoa

Boy 5 (*to Pedlar*) Here. How much?
Pedlar 2 Two marks.

Boy 5 takes a pie and pays the Pedlar

Ta.
Boy 6 (*to Boy 5*) Here, give us some. Come on!
Boy 7 What about us?
Boy 8 Come on. Pig!

A scuffle begins

Boy 8	)		(	Watch out!
Boy 6	}	(*together*)	{	Give us some!
Boy 9	)		(	What about me?

David rushes over

David (*breaking up the fight*) Stop it! Stop it! Leave him! (*To the Pedlar*)
I told you to clear off! Get out! Leave us alone! We don't want you! (*He
turns to Boy 5*) How much did you pay for that?
Boy 5 Two marks.
David Two marks? (*To the Pedlar*) You bloody thief!

The Pedlar has already gone

Boy 7 Ask him where he got the money from.
David We share our food here.
Boy 5 What food?
David Don't matter what it is! Everything goes in the coffer! (*Pause*) Did
you steal the money?
Boy 5 Yeah, I stole it. So what? They're rolling in money in that town!
Why shouldn't we have some?
Boy 9 Yeah. They never give us nothing.
David We beg!
Boy 5 You beg! I'm clearing off. This is stupid. What's so great about
being hungry every day? Eh?
Boy 9 I'm coming with you.
Boy 5 You lot can stay here! I'm going to make a living ... in Genoa!

Boy 5 and Boy 9 leave the camp

David watches them go

Nicholas and Francis in another part of the camp

Nicholas I'm tired.
Francis I know. (*Pause*) Nicholas, do you still think it's going to happen?
Nicholas Yes.
Francis When?
Nicholas Tomorrow.

Silence

Francis Perhaps we're in the wrong place.

Nicholas Do you think so?

Francis Well ... we can't stay here.

Nicholas Yes ... yes! It will happen farther down the coast! Thank you, Francis ... we'll move on.

Hugh Ferreus and William Porcus, two merchants, enter the camp. They appear rather comic, somewhat fussy and genteel

David What do you want? Who are you?

Ferreus We're from Genoa.

David Are you selling anything?

Ferreus No, not at all. Could you take us to Nicholas?

Porcus We hope to be of assistance to you.

David Come on ... over here.

He takes them to Nicholas and Francis. The following scene is in the presence of all the Crusaders

Nicholas, two men from Genoa. Merchants.

Nicholas Yes?

Ferreus Nicholas? We are from the city of Genoa. My name is Hugh Ferreus and this is my colleague, Mr Porcus. William Porcus.

Porcus How do you do?... Mr Ferreus and myself are in the business of shipping. Not in a big way. A little import and export ... mainly between here and Palermo. A small business you understand.

Ferreus (*gently*) Come to the point, William.

Porcus Well, we were so disgusted at the treatment you have received from our fellow citizens that we have decided to place at your disposal ... five vessels!

Ferreus Five of our finest, most reliable vessels.

Francis Wait a minute ... we haven't got any money.

Ferreus (*smiling*) We know that, we know that. (*Pause*) We are offering to take you to the Holy Land for nothing. Free of charge.

Francis Free? For no money?

Ad lib, excited reaction of Children

David Why?

Ferreus We are Christian men ... It is the least we can do, for the Glory of God.

Porcus It is our duty to help you.
Ferreus We both believe in your cause, and we gladly make this sacrifice.
Which after all is a small sacrifice when compared to your own. (*Pause*)
Well?

Ad lib, reaction of Children

Nicholas Wait! Wait a moment! Quiet. (*Pause*) Gentlemen, we thank you
for your offer ... but, may we have a little time to consider?
Ferreus Of course. Of course. No hurry ... come and see us tomorrow ...
our card. (*He gives a card to Nicholas*)
Porcus Thank you for receiving us.
Ferreus We look forward to seeing you in the morning. Come along,
William.
Nicholas Thank you.
Francis Thank you. Thank you.
Ferreus Thank *you*.

They exit in silence

Francis That's it! That's it! Nicholas, that's it!
Nicholas No!!

Sudden silence

Francis But ... that's what we wanted.
Nicholas We can't go. It's not the miracle.
Francis Oh! *Sod the miracle!*... We've got to get there!

Pause

Nicholas You don't believe.
Francis I do.
Nicholas You never believed.
Francis Nicholas ... please.
Nicholas You don't understand, do you, Francis?
Francis You need me, Nicholas.
Nicholas I need God!
Francis You need me! (*Pause*) You want to fail, don't you?... That's it,
isn't it?... You want to fail.

Pause

Nicholas I don't need you, Francis. I never have.
Francis Oh!... I want you to come with me.
Nicholas (*coldly*) Why?

*Pause. Francis turns away from Nicholas, he looks at the Children who
have been watching this "split"*

Francis (*to the Children*) We've been offered five ships. We have to take
them. We must get to Jerusalem. That's what we came for! We've
waited ... we've waited ... and ... now ... I believe that this is the miracle.
It is. We can't stay here any longer. I'm going to Jerusalem.

*As Francis makes this speech he walks through the camp until finally he
is on the other side of the acting area facing Nicholas*

Nicholas No! God will tell us. He will tell us when it is *right* for us to go.
The sea will open and we shall walk to the Holy Cross. That will be the
sign! Perhaps not here ... perhaps not here ... we shall move on, to
another town. But it will happen. It will happen. We must wait. It is
God's will that we should wait! This is not the miracle!
Francis Stay if you want to ... come if you want to ... I'm going.

Francis exits

Nicholas turns and exits in the opposite direction

*General ad lib from the Children as they decide what to do. The theme
music from the "Genoa" song is introduced. The discussion builds.
Lovers break up. Brothers and sisters part. Above the noise someone
shouts "Come on!". The Crusade has split into two factions.*

David exits with Nicholas

SCENE 10

Genoa — The law of supply and demand

The office of Mr Ferreus and Mr Porcus

Mr Ferreus is checking the final arrangements. Mr Porcus is calculating the possible profit based on a previous transaction. The mood of the scene should be busy, cold and efficient. The audience would find it almost incomprehensible

Ferreus (*going through some papers*) Where are they? Where are the stowage plans?

Clerk 1 Here.

Porcus Look up the record of the transaction last year with Vilfredo Borghese. April. That should give us some idea of the profit cost ratio.

Clerk 2 Right, sir.

Ferreus (*to Clerk 1*) We shall require the maximum diversification of cargo throughout all ships, allowing for any loss or delay *en route*. You must supervise that yourself.

Clerk 2 (*to Porcus*) Here you are, sir. (*He gives Porcus a ledger*)

Clerk 1 (*to Ferreus*) The Bills of Lading and the ship's manifest will be checked, sir.

Ferreus We've obtained Port clearance?

Clerk 1 No demurrage.

Porcus (*to Clerk 2*) The quantities don't really compare.

Clerk 2 Nor the quality!

Ferreus (*to Clerk 1*) What about the ship's chandlers?... Have we issued the advance notes?

Clerk 1 That's all in hand, sir ... here. (*He hands over some papers*)

Ferreus A thousand marks!

Clerk 1 We thought it advisable to strengthen each crew.

Ferreus I see. Good.

Porcus Port and Harbour dues ... well, we can multiply that by ten.

Clerk 2 (*to Porcus*) One month later and we'd be into the winter rates.

Porcus Two thousand, five hundred Nomizmahs ... what's the exchange rate?

Clerk 2 It's different now, sir.

Porcus What was it then?

Clerk 2 goes to look it up

Clerk 3 enters

Clerk 3 (*giving papers to Ferreus*) Applications for letters of credit, sir.
Ferreus (*signing them*) I take it these are for Palermo and Bougie.
Clerk 3 Yes.
Ferreus Get them to the bank straight away.

Clerk 3 exits at speed

Clerk 2 (*returning to Porcus with exchange rates*) Here you are, Mr
Porcus. Any tariffs will be *ad valorem.* It's impossible to estimate how
much each shipload might make at auction.
Ferreus (*to Porcus*) I've instructed Pettrochi regarding the reserve price
per head, but suggested he makes all the arrangements himself as he
knows the market.
Porcus (*to Ferreus*) His commission depends on it so we're in safe hands.
Clerk 2 I insisted on records and documents of all transactions just to be
on the safe side.
Porcus Good.

Clerk 4 enters

Clerk 4 Mr Ferreus ... what are the instructions for the return cargo?
Ferreus (*rummaging through papers*) Pettrochi is to use the money to
purchase silks, damasks, glass, muslin ...
Clerk 2 Here we are, sir. (*He hands a copy of instructions to Ferreus*)
Ferreus Thank you. Who's it for?
Clerk 4 The Ship's Master.
Ferreus (*giving Clerk 4 the papers*) All ships will remain in Port until
fully laden. There's no possibility of any returning under-ballast ... quite
the contrary in fact ... we may charter more vessels for the return.

Clerk 4 exits with papers

Porcus (*to Ferreus*) Any capital we have to play with will be in dinars,
Mr Ferreus.
Ferreus Yes, perhaps it would be wiser to make arrangements with our
bank in Alexandria ... (*To Clerk 1*) Make a note of that.

Clerk 1 exits

Porcus Well, it's difficult to compare with Cyprus ... but at this rate we could afford to lose four of the vessels and still be in credit. We can't lose.

Ferreus I don't intend to lose any ships ... or any of the cargo. This transaction is a golden opportunity for us to expand our trade in Africa.

Porcus Well, the initial outlay is minimal ... our return on investment should be quite staggering.

Ferreus Provided the children turn up.

Porcus They'll turn up.

SCENE 11

South of Pisa — The question of tactics

A Bandit is in the pillory. Schoolboys are throwing mud at him. If the Bandit could be chained to a wall like a dog on a lead, this would allow him some movement. The mud-throwing may be mimed

Bandit Come on, you Latin-scholars! Can't you do any better than that? You mincing milk-sops.

Boy 1 My! The fellow's a foul-mouth.

Boy 2 Shut your gob, you drunken pig!

Boy 3 He understood that!

Bandit Come on, snot-nose ... let me spit in your face!

Boy 1 Take a lesson from your betters, fatguts!

Boy 2 Learn some manners, rat face!

Boy 3 He's not so brave now is he? What's the matter, Bandit? Had enough?

Boy 1 Watch this ... right on his nose.

Boy 2 Missed! Come here ... I'll show you.

Boy 3 I'm next.

Bandit Come nearer ... you'll miss from there! Come nearer so I can spew on you.

Boy 2 Save that for tomorrow when they cut your guts open.

Boy 3 Yes. Then we'll see what a thief's made of!

Bandit You get a good look tomorrow when my innards gush out. You be there! You'll see my kidneys dance! You'll see some blood. Inside my belly I've got ropes, red ropes to strangle little bastards like you!

Boy 1 You don't frighten us, you wind-bag.

Boy 3 Watch your language, peasant! In front of gentlemen!

*The Crusaders enter with Nicholas and David. They are demoralized
after their failure at Pisa. They no longer have the chair with them*

Crusader 1 Leave him alone! Leave him alone!
Boy 1 I say ... look at this ragged bunch.
Crusader 2 Why are you doing this?
Boy 2 He's a thief, a bandit, we're teaching him some manners.
Boy 3 He'll be dead tomorrow. They're going to cut his innards out and
hang him up.
David Clear off! Leave him alone!
Bandit Who's this? Wipe the muck out of my eyes so I can see you!

Nicholas does so

David Go on! Clear off, you educated bastards!
Crusader 1 Get going!
Crusader 2 Go on! Shove off!
Boy 1 ⎧   ⎫ We're not afraid of you.
Boy 2 ⎨ (*together*) ⎬ We'll be back! We'll be back.
Boy 3 ⎩   ⎭ Crusaders! Ha! Ha!

The Schoolboys run off

Nicholas (*to the Bandit*) It's all right, they've gone now.
Bandit What are you lot doing here? Did you get fed up waiting for the
sea to open? Did they kick you out of Pisa?
Nicholas Is it true you will be executed tomorrow?
Bandit Which one of you is Nicholas?
Nicholas I am Nicholas.
Bandit Well, thanks for driving the flies away. But you needn't have
bothered. I was enjoying their attentions. This is my last impression of
the world and I want it to be an accurate one. I shall take the stench of
this foul place with me to the grave!
Crusader 4 Why are you so full of hate?
Crusader 5 Please, sir, make your peace with God.
Bandit *God* ...! I don't want you preaching at me. Who do you think you
are? What do you know? Nothing!
Crusader 5 We know blasphemy when we hear it.
Bandit What patronizing little pricks you are! Clear off! Send the other

little bastards back. I'd sooner have the muck that they throw at me! Go back to your mothers, you little dreamers, you know nothing. You've seen the filth, the violence, the corruption of the world and you know nothing!

Crusader 6 We know more than you think!

Bandit Dreamers! Chasing after miracles! Your God has deserted you. There is no God! There are no miracles! Just vermin, living on vermin!

Crusader 7 You're vermin!

Bandit That's right I am! I am a bandit! I fight force with force.

Crusader 7 And look where it got you!

Bandit Look at yourselves ... if you dare! You kids are a laughing-stock. No threat to your enemies, no help to your friends. You're useless!

Crusader 7 At least we didn't end up like you.

Bandit You'll never end up like me! You're not doing anything. They can ignore you!... Go home! You've made your feeble protest ... now go and join the merchants who you pretend to oppose ... get yourselves a job, like the rest of 'em who deserted you! You need guts to fight 'em, not dreams! The world's laughing at you! Go home!

Crusader 7 You bastard! We should have left you to the kids! (*He throws mud at the Bandit*)

Bandit Missed! You feeble sods ... you can't even do that right! There's no hope for you! *Go home!*

Crusader 6 Shut up! Shut up! Shut your mouth. (*He throws some mud*)

Bandit Come on, throw some more! At last! At last! Now you're doing something! Now we see whose side you're on!

Crusader 6 You asked for it!

Crusader 7 Thief! Bandit!

Crusader 8 Here you are, you bastard!

David Stop it! Stop it! He's right! Leave him alone.

Bandit Come on! Don't listen to him!... Serve your masters!

They stop throwing mud, and listen to David

David Look at us ... Look at what we're doing! This man is not our enemy!

Crusader 8 He's a bandit!

David So, what does a bandit do? He can't rob you, you haven't got anything! Look what happened to us at Genoa ... Look what happened at Pisa. The Crusade is over. You know it is. You're just waiting for someone to tell you to go home. Well, he's told you, I'm telling you ... go home!

Crusader 7 Nicholas, what can we do?

David We've been bloody idiots ... No-one's helped us, the Church hasn't helped us. "God" hasn't helped us. Everything we've done, we've done on our own. But where has it got us? We haven't changed anything!

Crusader 8 Perhaps we should have gone with Francis.

David No! What can he do? Nothing! Even if he gets to the Holy Land, he can't do anything. They've got the power, they can do what they want! ... Why should they listen to us? It's laughable! We couldn't even get across the sea. The merchants cross the sea every day. They don't need God to do it. They've got ships. They've got money! They've got power!

Bandit Stop shouting your mouth off, you. If you want to do something ... get me out of here.

David Come on!

Bandit I'll show you how to fight the bastards.

Crusaders 1, 2, 3 and 9 help David release the Bandit

Nicholas No! We can't use violence! We know the world is an evil place ... but we must oppose it with peace! ... Otherwise we're no better than they are.

Bandit There speaks a loser, if ever I heard one!

Nicholas I don't understand what went wrong.

Bandit Just make up your mind whose side you're on. But don't take too long about it, the world won't wait for your answer.

Crusader 6 What do we do, Nicholas?

Nicholas We can't break our vows. We must go to Rome.

Crusader 6 And then?

Nicholas Home.

David You can do what you want, Nicholas. I didn't come all this way, just to go home.

Bandit Come on, if you're coming.

David Goodbye, Nicholas.

Nicholas Goodbye.

The Crusade divides. One by one the Crusaders leave Nicholas to join the Bandit and David. Nicholas is left with a handful of followers

They exit

SCENE 12

Bougie — money talks

The slave auction at Bougie

The Girls sit in a group waiting to be sold. The Boys, including Francis, are also on stage. All the Children are in chains and are dressed in minimal clothing

The Auctioneer and the Buyers return from lunch for the afternoon session. Ad lib conversations as they enter. The Buyers take up their positions and observe the scene with clinical detachment

Auctioneer (*at maximum speed with minimum energy*) Lot three hundred and one, gentlemen. Consignment from Porcus and Ferreus of Genoa. Lot three hundred and one, seven female slaves. You will notice that as with previous examples of this shipment, no attempt has been made on the part of Pettrochi to in any way deceive or mislead potential buyers. Such is the confidence he has in his merchandise that they are presented to you ... unwashed, unkempt and generally in a state of disorder. They are, in fact, gentlemen, straight off the boat. Straight off the boat and yet unsurpassed in beauty. How do we do it? Gentlemen, you are looking at "quality". Natural quality! Come here.

Girl 1 steps forward

North European origin. Black hair. No lice. No physical defects. A perfect specimen. Fourteen years old and untouched by human hand. A virgin you have my word on that. A lovely face, a lovely figure, and lovely skin. Soft white skin. Proud little breasts. What more can I say? Nothing. Those thighs speak for theirselves. Back.

Girl 2 steps forward

And as if that wasn't enough. Come here. Same country of origin. Same quality. Blonde hair. Look at that face, gentlemen. Demure is the word I'm groping for. You are witnessing charm the like of which is unprecedented. And on top of that she is endowed with certain attributes which enhance her value. I'm thinking of the kitchen now, a very handy little cook is this one. You!

Girl 3 steps forward

Take a look at that. Walk around. Words are superfluous, I could go home now. What's racing through your minds now, gentlemen, is the question of child-bearing. Correct me if I'm wrong. What you see before you was designed for that purpose. Fifteen years old and unbelievably enough ... yet another virgin. Keep walking. Smile a little. Exude some confidence. That's better. Now a critic might say that that is on the skinny side. I prefer to call it feline. Graceful, that's what she is, graceful. Takes your breath away, don't it? Well, that's enough of that. Musn't have too much of what we fancy. Don't do that, sir, you'll go blind. (*To the Girl*) Sit down. Give us a rest. Ha. Ha. What have we here? Stand up, and you. Up, up.

Two girls stand up

Two delightful miniatures. Feast your eyes on them. Collector's pieces they are, gentlemen. Not only are they tantalizing, they are also very useful to have around. Very good with a needle these two, stitch away all day they will. Make anything. Make good presents as a matter of fact. You could give 'em away to your business associates. A gift for a visiting Sultan perhaps. What a bargain they are, gentlemen. Sit down. Well, they're beautiful, they're intelligent, hard-working and healthy. You've got embroiderers, domestics, cooks and concubines and all I'm asking for 'em is ... money! Now who's going to start us off at ten thousand dinars? Gentleman over there. Thank you. Fifteen, fifteen, twenty. Twenty-five. Twenty-five. Thirty. Thirty-five. Thirty-five. Forty. Forty thousand dinars. Any advance on forty thousand dinars? Forty-two? Thank you, sir, forty-two. Forty-five. Forty-seven. Forty-seven. Forty-eight. Forty-nine. Fifty. Fifty thousand dinars. Any advance on fifty thousand dinars? Against you, sir. Any more bids? Any more bids? Sold for fifty thousand dinars, gentleman on my left. (*To the Girls*) Who you'll be pleased to know is a Christian, so you're in good hands. Fifty thousand dinars, subject to physical examination ... and that alone should be worth the price. Sold to the Frank. Lot three hundred and two.

The Clerk records the transaction. The next lot is brought forward, ten Boys who include Francis

Lot three hundred and two, ten male slaves. Once again, gentlemen, there has been no attempt by Mr Pettrochi, to wash up, brush up, feed up or build up any of these articles. You have my personal guarantee on that. What you see is what you buy. Ten male slaves. All under sixteen, all European, all white. What more could you want? Come here.

Boy 1 steps forward. He should be the Boy who sang "The Sea" in Act I

Pretty, don't you think? Notice the hair. The skin. Lovely to look at and more besides. A song bird he is. Got a voice on him that would send shivers up your spine. I won't ask him for a demonstration now in case I lose control and buy him myself. Take my word for it, gentlemen, he is magic, unadulterated magic. You!

A Boy with ginger hair steps forward

Deceptive this one. Unusual colouring and that in itself lends a certain novelty value to him. Is he strong? I hear you ask. Take a look at them muscles. Come on, show 'em, show us your muscles. He's got muscles in places where I haven't even got places. And what a worker! You name it, he'll do it. As a matter of fact he'll *do* anything, if you understand my meaning. He has a reputation as a ram. Very virile. When you buy this one you buy youself a generation or two. In fact he's so virile, you buy him and you could put me out of business and set up on your own. Sit down before I say too much. You!

Francis steps forward

Recommend this one for heavy work. A bit of gardening perhaps, digging, lifting, carrying things about. He likes to be kept on the go. Very healthy he is. Look at his teeth. Come on, show us your teeth. There. He's got an engaging smile on him, don't you think? You should smile more often. I think you'll find him very loyal and very reliable. He has a warm quality which I find very appealing. Down.

Francis sits

Ah yes. Now, how about this for beauty?

Another Boy steps forward

Gentlemen, you are looking at a cherub and you don't need me to tell you what you can use him for. Sit down. And that's not all, they can dance, they can run, they can entertain and amuse. Go!

Another Boy displays his acrobatic skill

Ain't he amazing, gentlemen? And again, go!

The Boy repeats the exercise

What a lovely mover he is. A lovely little mover. Wonderful, wonderful. That's enough. Get back. Very eager to please they are, very eager. I make no claims for this one.*(Indicating another Boy)* As you can see he ain't up to much. A bit on the weak side. Not very bright. But then again you can't have everything, I point him out to let you know we've got nothing to hide. Right then, lot three hundred and two. Who's going to start us off at the ridiculously low price of fifteen thousand dinars? Gentleman over there. Thank you. Fifteen. Twenty. Twenty. Twenty-five. Twenty-five. Thirty. Thirty. Thirty-five. Thirty-five. Thirty-eight? Thirty-eight, forty? Forty thousand dinars. Any advance on forty thousand dinars? Come along now, gentlemen, you can always throw that weak one away. Forty thousand dinars. Do I hear forty-two? Thank you. Forty-three? Forty-three. Forty-five. Forty-six. Forty-seven. Forty-seven thousand dinars. Any advance on forty-seven thousand dinars? Against you, sir. Any more bids? Any more bids? Forty-seven thousand dinars ... going ... going ... Sold to the agent for the Sultan Al Kamil for forty-seven thousand dinars. *(To the boys)* Nothing but the best for you lads. Forty-seven thousand dinars, subject to physical examination. Sold to the Sultan of Egypt. Lot number three hundred and three!

Song: Who Can You Trust?

Slaves   Who can you trust, if not in other men?
                    They needed us, we never needed them.

How did we fail? We were naïve kids.
Now we are for sale, for the highest bids.

Who can you trust, if not in other men?
They needed us, we never needed them.

You just cannot trust — in other men.

SCENE 13

Rome — Pope Innocent III discovers the source of new recruits

Nicholas and the remaining Crusaders enter

Crusader 1 Well, I'll say this for it ... it's big.
Crusader 2 Ssh!

Pause

Crusader 3 I wonder what he looks like.

Six Cardinals enter, followed by the Pope

Nicholas (*after a long pause*) Are you the Pope?
Pope Are you Nicholas?

Pause

Nicholas Why did God let us down?

Shocked reaction from the Cardinals. The Pope smiles

Pope We were led to believe your reputation was for eloquence, not for
  plain-speaking.
Nicholas He said the sea would open, and it didn't.

Pause

Pope Nicholas ... Who said the sea would open?

Nicholas God ... well, Jesus.

Pope Really?

Nicholas I saw Him.

Pope My child, sometimes we *think* we see things which we don't really see. Sometimes the things we see are not what they appear to be. They may even be the opposite to their appearance. Who can tell? You think that you saw Jesus ... but we think you are the victim of a most cruel deception. Are you aware that the devil can manifest himself in the guise of an angel?

Nicholas I saw Jesus.

Pope You are mistaken! Before setting out on your journey, you would have been well-advised to seek the counsel of a priest or someone in authority. You might then have avoided the error, or indeed the sin, of presumptuousness. Nicholas, do you know what "vanity" is?

Nicholas Yes.

Pope Only a vain person would presume to do what you have done ... to test the existence of God in this manner. My child, you have over-reached yourself and the price of your vanity is your failure. It is not God who has failed you, but rather you who have failed God!

Nicholas We have lost our faith. We have walked ... walked from Cologne to Genoa ... from Genoa to Rome ... and we have lost our faith.

Pope Pray to God to forgive you, and your faith will be restored.

Nicholas Release us from our vows ... please.

The Children kneel

Pope Were we to release you from your Crusading vows, we should be neglecting our duty towards you. You must not ask the shepherd to turn his back on his sheep. Rather we should seek to strengthen those ties, which even now bind us together. Return home, my son, we shall postpone the fulfilment of your vows until such time as your faith is restored to you. (*He Pope turns to go*)

Nicholas Then it was all for nothing.

The Pope stops. He turns round to Nicholas

Pope No, Nicholas, your journey was not for nothing. For you have revealed to us the great multitude who seek to support our cause. You have shown us the common people who look to us for leadership. As a

consequence of your actions we are preparing a new Crusade, calling
upon all Christians, regardless of wealth or status, to become — Soldiers
of Christ!

*The next passage is an echo of Scene 1. Each statement should be
punctuated by the crash of a gong*

Cardinal 1 We shall hold magnificent processions, every month!

Cardinal 2 In order to intercede with God for the deliverance of the Holy
Land!

Cardinal 3 This Crusade shall be inspired with a vigorous and fervent
leadership!

Cardinal 4 Which shall not permit the wicked intervention of the secular
powers!

Cardinal 5 We shall drive the foul Infidel from the Holy Land!

Cardinal 6 We shall liberate the Holy Sepulchre!

Cardinal 1 We shall see, at last, the final victory of the Christian Church!

Pause

Pope (*quietly*) Your journey, my son, was not for nothing. Return home,
and await our call.

The Pope and the Cardinals exit

Song: Who Can You Trust?

Crusaders   In God we trusted, we believed in Him.
He needed us, we never needed Him.

Our faith is gone. We stand alone.
The road is long, that leads us back home.

In God we trusted, we believed in Him.
He needed us, we never needed Him.

You just cannot trust — in faith alone.

Scene 14

Near Pisa — the Good Samaritan

An injured man lies beside the road. Two Pilgrims are with him. One attends to his wounds. The other is praying for his recovery. The scene is a trap, prepared by the Bandits, for a merchant. One of the "Pilgrims" is David. It is night

Pilgrim 1 *(praying quietly, mumbling)* Bow down thine ear, O Lord, and hear me; for I am poor and in misery. Preserve thou my soul for I am holy: my God save thy servant that putteth his trust in thee. Be merciful unto me, O Lord: for I will call daily unto thee. Comfort the soul of thy servant: for unto thee, O Lord, do I lift up my soul. For thou, Lord, art good and gracious: and of great mercy unto all them that call upon thee. Give ear, Lord, unto my prayer: and ponder the voice of my humble desires. In the time of my trouble I will call upon thee: for thou hearest me...

A Merchant enters on horseback. (In the NYT production we did not use a horse. Instead two actors were used as "carriers" and the dialogue was changed accordingly.) He is a small business man on his way from Rome to the Champagne fair at Provins. He has two sacks containing dyes, spices, silks and copperware

David *(dressed as a pilgrim)* Stop! Stop! Sir, please help us.

The Merchant stops

Praise God for your arrival, friend ... this man is dying.
Merchant Stay where you are. Don't come any nearer!
Pilgrim 1 We are pilgrims, friend, on our way to Rome. We found this man by the roadside. He has been attacked by bandits. Please help us.
Merchant How far is it to Pisa?
Pilgrim 1 Not far. An hour on horseback.
Merchant I'll ride into Pisa and send you a physician. *(He prepares to go)*
David No sir. Please! Please help us. This man may die. I appeal to you ... as a Christian. Please take him with you.

Pilgrim 1 I fear for his life, sir. He may not last the hour.

The Merchant hesitates

David If we could lift him on to your horse, we may yet be in time to save him. For God's sake man, he's dying!

The Merchant dismounts

Merchant Let's have a look.
David Thank you, sir. You're a good man.

All three crouch over the body

The Bandits enter from all sides. The lead the horse away a little and stand by the Merchant

Merchant Who are you?... What?... Oh God, save us!

David, Pilgrim 1 and the Injured Man reveal themselves to be with the Bandits

No!... Oh God!

The Bandits are going through the sacks. They pull out large pieces of silk in bright red and blue

No please, not that, don't take that please ... please. I'm a poor man. I have a wife.
Bandit 1 What's this?
Merchant They're dyes. They're no use to you. Dyes for cloth. Please ... here take these ... take these. (*He takes out copper-ware, pots and plates*) Look, it's copper ... you can sell these. You'll get a good price for them. Take these.
Bandit 2 Plates. Pots.
Merchant Listen to me ... please ... I'm not a rich man! This is everything I have. I've spent all my money ... in Rome. I must get these to the Champagne Fair at Provins!
Bandit 3 What's this?

Merchant No!... Spices ... cinnamon ... mace ... pepper, I must sell them!
This is my whole life. My future. Please listen. If you take all these, my
wife and I will have nothing. Nothing. We're poor people. This was our
chance ... Just take the copper ... We saved up, we borrowed money!
Please ... I'm begging you ... Just the copper.
David No! Go now, before we kill you.
Bandit leader Go on. Run.
Merchant My horse.
Bandit leader Run!
Merchant Oh God!

He runs off

Bandit leader If you give in to the bastards they'll have you!

Song: Who Can You Trust

Bandits   Who can you trust, if you're to stay alive?
The world is hard, and everyday's a fight.

No-one will help, so don't you help them
They'll get you first, if you don't get them.

Who can you trust, if you're to stay alive?
The world is hard, and everyday's a fight.

Just trust yourselves. Then you'll survive.

SCENE 15

Cairo — the Crusade reaches its conclusion

A classroom

*The Teacher enters with the Slaves. The Slaves are immaculate, they are
well-dressed. They enter in a straight line and are each carrying a slate
and chalks*

Teacher Come along. Come along. This morning we shall be visited by the Sultan Al Kamil. This will be an informal inspection, and I would ask you to carry on working in the normal way. But please remember the etiquette that I have taught you. (*He indicates that they should sit*)

They sit cross-legged in neat rows. All their movements are executed with beautiful precision

I'm sure I can rely on you to make a good impression. Right. The volume of a truncated pyramid. One moment.

The teacher goes off to collect his visual aid: a model of a pyramid

At the back of the class, Francis is whispering

Francis This is our chance.
Boy 1 What?
Francis Al Kamil. I'm going to ask him.
Boy 1 Ask him what?
Francis For the Cross.
Boy 2 What's he saying?
Boy 3 What?
Boy 4 He's going to ask for the Cross.
Francis That's what we came for, we must ask him.
Boy 1 Leave off, we like it here!
Boy 3 (*to Francis*) You keep your mouth shut!

The Teacher returns with his model of a pyramid and a copy of the formula

Teacher Francis, I don't mind you talking, but please try not to disturb the rest of the class. (*Pause*) This is a pyramid. (*He removes the top section*) And this is a truncated pyramid. Now, to discover the volume of a truncated pyramid, that is to say, this section here, we shall require yet another formula. Right. Let us call the distance from the base to the intersection H. We shall call the length of the top line B. And the length of the bottom line A. So, at the top, we have a square of sides length B. And at the bottom we have a square of sides length A. And the distance between the two is H. Now, we shall call the volume P. The volume of a truncated pyramid then, is given by the following formula ... P equals

H over three, open brackets. A square, plus AB, plus B square, close brackets. Any questions? Yes, Stephen.

Boy 4 What use is it?

Teacher That's a good question. Geometry is of practical use to builders and architects, to them it is an economic necessity. Now, copy down the formula. P equals H over three, open brackets, A squared, plus ——

The Sultan Al Kamil enters

The Teacher bows

Yasidi.

The Slaves stand and bow. When the bow is completed, they sit. Once again they move with precision

Al Kamil How are they progressing?

Teacher Quite well. Quite well.

Al Kamil (*to Boy 5*) Are you finding the work difficult?

Boy 5 No, not at all. Well ... sometimes.

Al Kamil But you're quite happy?

Boy 5 Oh yes. Yes thank you.

Al Kamil Good.

Teacher Simon here is our most promising pupil.

But Al Kamil ignores this, he goes to Boy 6

Al Kamil (*to Boy 6*) And you. Do you find your room comfortable?

Boy 6 Sorry?... Oh yes. Very.

Francis (*standing*) Sultan.

Al Kamil Yes?

Francis We are pilgrims, Christians, from Cologne in Germany. We set out in peace to reach you. Please give us the Holy Cross. (*Pause*) Our journey has been very hard, very difficult, many of us have died, it has taken us a long while to get here. But we *are* here. You rule over our Holy City, please give it back to us.

Al Kamil (*gently*) No.

Francis I'll do whatever you ask. If you want me to bear witness to my faith ... I'll put my hands in the flames. Anything. We have come for Jerusalem.

A long pause. Al Kamil replies in a gentle manner

Al Kamil I'm sorry. We are from different countries, we have different religions. I shall make no attempt to convert you. But for a Muslim, Jerusalem is a Holy City. It is the farthest place of prostration. It was from there that the Great Prophet Mohammed ——
Francis It is a Christian City! Give it to us!
Al Kamil (*quietly*) What's your name?
Francis Francis. Please ... I have led these people ... I brought them here. I promised that I would take them to the Holy Land ... I promised ... to God. Please ... we are soldiers of peace.
Al Kamil You are nothing but slaves. And your behaviour is a disgraceful reflection upon your teacher. You are no longer pilgrims, you are slaves. If you had been purchased by a Christian you would be suffering in the sugar plantations of Cyprus. (*Pause*) Consider yourselves very lucky that you are ... my slaves.

Al Kamil turns to the Teacher. The Teacher bows

Teacher I'm sorry. I apologize.

Al Kamil exits slowly

The Slaves stand, they all bow. One of the boys hits Francis. Francis falls to the ground

(*To Francis*) You idiot! Who do you think you are? Your religion is of no use to you here! How dare you address the Sultan like that? You are slaves! You have no rights! (*Pause*) That's enough. Return to your rooms. All of you. In silence please! I am a patient man. Patient.

They exit

SCENE 16

Cologne — a rumour of no consequence

The town square in Cologne

All the Parents enter. They enter in small groups and take up positions around the acting areas. They are talking in whispers, waiting for their Children to return. They are frightened. Nicholas's Father stands c, alone. Almost the entire company is on stage. There should be the steady beat of a drum throughout this scene

Finally, Nicholas enters with the remnants of the Crusade, about six Boys. They look for their parents. They rush to them. Nicholas runs into his father's arms. We become aware of the many parents, who have lost their children. The following lines come from all around the acting area

Parent 1 (*to Nicholas*) Why did you come back?
Parent 2 What's happened to my boys?
Parent 3 It's our fault for letting them go in the first place.
Parent 4 They must have died in the mountains.
Parent 5 He must be safe. He must be alive.
Parent 6 They ought to be hanged for what they've done.
Parent 2 Dear God, what's happened to my boys?
Parent 7 Did she reach the sea?
Parent 8 Did he get to Genoa?
Parent 9 That's him. That's Nicholas's father.
Parent 10 What happened to my children?
Parent 11 No. No. They were sold as slaves.
Parent 12 (*to Nicholas*) You must remember my daughter.
Parent 1 (*to Nicholas*) You killed my son!
Parent 13 Leave him alone! Leave him!
Parent 12 (*to Nicholas*) You knew what you were doing. Didn't you? You
   knew!
Parent 14 He knew all right. They paid him.
Parent 15 He's to blame.
Parent 16 He arranged it.
Parent 17 How much did they pay you?
Parent 18 Yeah! How much?
Parent 19 He sold them.
Parent 9 He sold them into slavery.
Parent 20 Murderer!
Parent 21 We ought to kill him.
Parent 22 We ought to lynch him.

Parent 23 Kill him.
Parent 24 Kill him.
Parent 25 Kill him.
Parent 26 Slavery, he sold them into slavery!
Parent 27 He did.
Parent 2 He'll burn in hell!
Parent 28 This is the work of the devil!

They begin to move towards Nicholas

Parent 16 Kill him!
Parent 29 He killed them!
Parent 20 Hang him!
Parent 30 Kill him!
All Parents Kill him! Kill him! Kill him! Kill him! Kill him!

Parent 13, a mother, rushes to protect Nicholas

Parent 13 (*shouting*) No! For God's sake, don't kill another child!

The Parents hesitate

Parent 31 All right then, get the father.
Parent 24 He knew all along.
Parent 32 They paid him.
Parent 33 The slave traders, Ferreus and Porcus.
Parent 34 Hugh the Iron and William the Pig!
Parent 20 He's the one. Get the father!
Parent 35 It was all set up!
Parent 36 Of course it was!
Parent 16 Kill him!

All the Parents move towards Nicholas's Father

All Parents Kill him! Kill him! Kill him! Kill him! Kill him! Kill him!
(*shouting*) For God's sake kill him!

The Parents hang Nicholas's Father. The drumbeat stops. Silence. They look at what they have done. The body is taken down after the first verse of the last song

Song: If We Only Have Love

Girl (solo)	If we only have love.
	That is what we believed.
	So we only had love.
	And we didn't succeed.
Girls	You waved and you smiled,
Boys	When we were leaving,
Girls	You kissed your child,
Boys	When we were leaving.
Girls	You hoped that we might do what you have never done.
All	Well that's too bad!
	Because your child is just no better than anyone!
Girls	What shall we say,
Boys	To our own children?
All	Should we tell them that their lives have been arranged?

That would be true
If all we do
Is to give to them a world that can't be changed.
Our ideas were quite sound,
While they stayed in our head.
But they died on the ground,
Where the world turns around,
To the sound,
Of money talking.
While we were walking,
To the sound of money talking.
And in the end,
For all we have done,
We cannot give to anyone,
A world that cannot be changed.
A world that cannot be changed.

The world — it can be changed!

BLACK-OUT

FURNITURE AND PROPERTY LIST

ACT I
SCENE 1

No props required

SCENE 2

On stage: Nil

Off stage: Chair (Four **Boys**)

Personal: **Sebastian**: apple in pocket

SCENE 3

On stage: Plough and harnesses
Jackets, food (including loaf of bread), water

Off stage: Blankets, sack of grain (**Klaus**)

SCENE 4

On stage: Nil

Off stage: Bread, blankets (**Children**)
Chair (**Attendants**)
Lighted lantern (**Francis**)

SCENE 5

No props required

SCENE 6

On stage: Nil

Off stage: Chair (**Attendants**)
Cudgels, scythes, pitchforks (**Peasants**)

SCENE 7

On stage:	Nil
Personal:	**Bishop**: ring

SCENE 8

On stage:	Chair
Personal:	**Bishop**: ring

ACT II
SCENE 9

Genoa:

On stage:	Nil
Off stage:	Ladder, sack (**Steve, Patrick**)
	Copper jug (**Peter**)
Personal:	**Merchant**: purse

Camp:

On stage:	Chair
	Coffer
Off stage:	Money (**Marian**)
	Money (**Stephanie**)
	Tray with buns and cakes (**Pedlar 1**)
	Tray with meat pies (**Pedlar 2**)
Personal:	**Boy 5**: money
	Ferreus: card

SCENE 10

On stage:	Desks with papers, ledgers, pens, ink, etc.
Off stage:	Papers (**Clerk 3**)

SCENE 11

On stage: Pillory or chains

SCENE 12

On stage: Nil

Personal: **Children:** chains
                  Auctioneer: pen, paper

SCENE 13

No props required

SCENE 14

On stage: Nil

Off stage: Horse, sacks containing dyes, spices, silks, copperware
                  (**Merchant**)

SCENE 15

On stage: Nil

Off stage: Slates, chalks (**Slaves**)
                  Model of truncated pyramid, copy of formula (**Teacher**)

SCENE 16

On stage: Nil

Off stage: Rope (**Parent**)

LIGHTING PLOT

Property fittings required: lighted lantern

ACT I

To open: Lighting on **Cardinals**

Cue 1	The **Old Crusader** enters *Spot on* **Old Crusader**	(Page 1)
Cue 2	The **Old Crusader** exits *Cross-fade to lighting on* **Children**	(Page 2)
Cue 3	As various groups meet for leave-takings *Spot on each group as it speaks*	(Page 4-7)
Cue 4	As **Old Crusader** exits *Cross-fade to lighting on farm*	(Page 8)
Cue 5	**Farmer** and **Klaus** exit *Cross-fade to evening lighting on Alps, with lighted lantern for* **Francis**	(Page 12)
Cue 6	**Francis:** "Get some sleep." *Fade lighting further; spot on* **Nicholas** and **Francis**	(Page 16)
Cue 7	**Francis** puts his head in **Nicholas's** lap *Fade spot slowly; continue to fade lighting slowly to night*	(Page 16)
Cue 8	**Nicholas's Father** examines sleeping children *Light on* **Cardinals**	(Page 19)
Cue 9	Laughter suddenly stops *Black-out*	(Page 20)
Cue 10	When ready *Spot on* **Nicholas,** *spreading light as dawn breaks*	(Page 20)

Cue 11	**Child** takes shoes from corpse and exits	(Page 21)
	Cross-fade to lighting on **Cardinals**	
Cue 12	**Pope:** "We do nothing."	(Page 23)
	Cross-fade to lighting on fields	
Cue 13	**Children** work in total silence, with no co-ordination,	
	no pleasure	(Page 27)
	Cross-fade to lighting on Senate	
Cue 14	**Senator:** "... we are the ones responsible!"	(Page 31)
	Cross-fade to spot on **Boy** *singing, gradually increasing*	
	to general lighting as other **Children** *join in*	
Cue 15	**Children** hold their positions in absolute silence	(Page 34)
	Very slow fade to Black-out	

ACT II

To open: Lighting on camp

Cue 16	At end of "Song of Survival"	(Page 36)
	Cross-fade to lighting on Genoa	
Cue 17	**Merchant** puts his arm around **Debbie**. They leave	(Page 40)
	Cross-fade to lighting on camp	
Cue 18	**David** exits with **Nicholas**	(Page 46)
	Cross-fade to lighting on office	
Cue 19	**Porcus:** "They'll turn up."	(Page 49)
	Cross-fade to lighting on pillory	
Cue 20	**Crusaders** exit	(Page 52)
	Cross-fade to lighting on slave auction	
Cue 21	**Slaves:** " ... in other men."	(Page 57)
	Cross-fade to lighting on **Crusaders** *and* **Cardinals**	
Cue 22	**Crusaders:** "... in faith alone."	(Page 59)
	Cross-fade to lighting on road to Pisa	

Cue 23	**Bandits**: "... Then you'll survive." *Cross-fade to classroom*	(Page 62)
Cue 24	**Slaves** exit from classroom *Cross-fade to town square*	(Page 65)
Cue 25	**All**: "The world — it can be changed!" *Black-out*	(Page 68)

EFFECTS PLOT

ACT I

Cue 1   During Scene 1   (Page 1)
Periodic loud bells and crashes of a gong

ACT II

Cue 2   As **Children** ad lib deciding what to do   (Page 46)
Music: theme from "Genoa" song; fade as
Crusaders *exit*

Cue 3   As **Cardinals 1-6** speak   (Page 59)
Crashes of a gong to punctuate their statements

Cue 4   During Scene 16   (Page 66)
Steady beat of drum throughout

Cue 5   **Parents** hang **Nicholas's Father**   (Page 67)
Stop drumbeats

NB Bell, gong, and drum effects may be performed live on stage

THE MUSIC FOR THE
CHILDREN'S CRUSADE
by
Robert Campbell

.

THE SONG OF THE CONFIDENCE OF YOUTH

THE SONG OF OVERCOMING DIFFICULTIES

♩ = 108

VERSE 1: There's not a thing that we don't know a-bout these moun-tains. We know that chil-dren cry when they're a - lone. We have learned to live in ter-ri-ble con - di-tions, But we learned that les-son long a - go at home.

VERSE 2: There's not a thing that we don't know a-bout these moun-tains. We've seen the stains of blood be-neath our feet, But we know that in the end when we have no-thing Our hope a - lone will keep us from de - feat.

1st CHORUS

Now it's cold oh, how the night is freez-ing, But there's no-thing we can do to al-ter that.

THE SONG OF FALSE CONCLUSIONS

THE SONG OF SURVIVAL

WHO CAN YOU TRUST?

IF WE ONLY HAVE LOVE

What shall we say — To our own chil-dren?

Should we tell them that their lives

have been ar-ranged? That would be true

If all we do Is to give to them

a world that can't be changed.

Our i - deas were quite sound, While they

stayed in our head. But they died on the ground,

Where the world turns a - round, To the

sound, of mo - ney talk - ing.___ While we___

___ were walk - ing,___ To the sound of mo -

- - ney talk- - ing. ___

And in the end,___ For all we have

done, We can-not give to a - ny - one,

A world_____ that can-not be changed.___

___ A world_____ that can-not be changed.___

___ The world - it can be changed!